UP THE POLL

GREAT IRISH ELECTION STORIES

Shane Coleman

Cartoons by Fintan Taite

MENTOR
BOOKS

First Published in 2007 by

MENTOR BOOKS
43 Furze Road
Sandyford Industrial Estate
Dublin 18
Republic of Ireland

Tel: + 353 1 295 2112 / 3   Fax: + 353 1 295 2114
e-mail: admin@mentorbooks.ie
www.mentorbooks.ie

© Shane Coleman

The views and opinions expressed in this book are entirely those of the contributors and do not necessarily reflect the views of the publisher. The publishers do not accept any responsibility for any loss or damage suffered by any person as a result of the information provided in this book.

All rights reserved. No part of this publication may be reproduced, stored in a retrieval system, or transmitted in any form or by any means electronic, mechanical, photocopying, recording, or otherwise, without prior written permission of the publisher.

ISBN: 978-1-84210-389-0

A catalogue record for this book
is available from the British Library

Editor: Treasa O'Mahony
Typesetting: Kathryn O'Sullivan
Cover Image & Text Illustrations: Fintan Taite www.fintantaite.com

Printed in Ireland by ColourBooks Ltd.
1 3 5 7 9 10 8 6 4 2

Foreword

Perhaps the tremendous passion for politics that has always existed in Ireland has cooled a little over the past twenty years, but general elections remain a serious spectator sport for Irish people. The one million plus people who watched the leaders' debate on television during the 2007 general election is evidence of that.

Up the Poll is an attempt to capture the excitement, tension, fervour, exhilaration, tragedy and humour that has been generated by elections. It is essentially a collection of individual, stand-alone election stories that, hopefully, when combined gives a comprehensive picture of the electoral history of the Irish State.

Some stories are light and whimsical, others are absolutely central to how the Irish political system has developed. Every election since the foundation of the State is covered in some shape or form and virtually every major political figure – along with more than a few minor ones too – features at some point.

I would like to thank my family and friends for their support when I was writing this book, most particularly Ev, Cúan and Donagh for their amazing patience and understanding.

Thanks also to Danny McCarthy at Mentor Books who came up with the original idea for this book; and to Treasa O'Mahony at Mentor for all her expert advice and help.

A special note of gratitude to Stephen Collins for enduring my constant picking of his considerable brain about elections past.

Thanks also to Michael Clifford and all my colleagues at *The Sunday Tribune*. Additional thanks to the staff at the National Library for their courtesy and professionalism.

Shane Coleman

September 2007

Acknowledgements

- Gill & MacMillan for *Breaking the Mould: How the PDs changed Irish Politics* by Stephen Collins; *All in a Life: An Autobiography* by Garret FitzGerald; *Seán Lemass* by Brian Farrell; *Irish Elections 1918-1977: Parties, Voters and Proportional Representation* by Cornelius O'Leary; *This is Charlie Bird* by Charlie Bird; *Against the Tide* by Noel Browne
- Poolbeg Press for *The Boss: Charles J Haughey in Government* by Joe Joyce and Peter Murtagh
- Cambridge University Press for *Ireland, 1912-1985: Politics and Society* by Joe Lee
- Dublin and London 1970 for *Eamon De Valera* by Lord Longford
- New Island Books for *Snakes & Ladders* by Fergus Finlay
- O'Brien Press for *People, Politics and Power – From O'Connell to Ahern* by Stephen Collins; *The Power Game: Ireland under Fianna Fáil* by Stephen Collins
- Political Studies Association of Ireland for *Irish Elections 1922 – 44: Results and Analysis* by Michael Gallagher; *Days of Blue Loyalty: the Politics of Membership of the Fine Gael Party* by Michael Gallagher and Michael Marsh
- Penguin Books Ltd for *A Secret History of the IRA* by Ed Moloney
- Irish Academic Press for *De Valera, Fianna Fáil and the Irish Press: The Truth in the News* by Mark O'Brien

Contents

1. Rumble in Ranelagh (1997 – 2007) 1
2. Now You Tree It, Now You Don't (1982) 10
3. Owen's Goal (2002) 14
4. Wrap the Red Flag 'Round Me (1985) 21
5. In the Shadow of the Gunmen (1922) 24
6. The Dullest Election (1961) 31
7. Three Hail Marys (1977 – 1987) 36
8. The Postman Knocked Once (Dublin Central – 1) (2007) . 41
9. I Deem the Candidate . . . Nicked (1923 – 1925) 46
10. The Ulimate Poll Topper (1923 – 1948) 52
11. Consulting the Stars (1977) 57
12. Up the Poll (2002) 63
13. The Agony and the Ex TD – 1 (1965) 68
14. The Agony and the Ex TD – 2 (1992) 74
15. Jack on the Box (1973) 80
16. Death on the Canvass – 1 (1932) 85
17. Cleaning Up After the Election (1932) 92
18. Fine Gael's Lowest Ebb (1945) 97
19. Inflation Once Again (1977) 104
20. Three Rounds of Charlie v Garret (1981 – 1987) 108
21. Vote Seán Phaddy Shéamus Number One (1944) 118
22. So Good They Elected him Twice (1927) 121
23. Death on the Canvass – 2 (1954) 126
24. Bad Timing (1932 – 1997) 129
25. I Deem the Candidate . . . Bankrupt (1927) 135
26. A Bad Day for Fine Gael (2002) 140
27. The Electorally Embarrassed (1923) 144

28. The 21 Lost Deputies (1923 – 1927) 148
29. It's a Long Count in Tipperary (1943) 151
30. Election? What Election? (1920) 155
31. The TDs Behind the Wire (1981) 158
32. The Gerrymanders (1930 – 1974) 162
33. The Most Bitter General Election (1933) 170
34. The Battle for Tang Church (1987) 175
35. The Twenty-Five County Dáil (2007) 181
36. Who Feared to Stand in '38 (1938) 184
37. Spring's Winter of Content (1982) 189
38. How Dev Bit the Bullet (1923) 196
39. Fianna Fáil's Record Breaker (1938) 200
40. Family Favourites (1959) 204
41. The Soldiers Fulfill Their Destiny (1932) 208
42. Put Him In to Get Him Out (1917) 214
43. Tipp's Top Tory (1790) 220
44. Playing the Green Card (1982) 225
45. Reds Under the Bed (1932 – 1969) 232
46. The Day Mickey Doherty Took a Pfennig
    Off the Pound (1992) 247
47. George 'Second Best' (Dublin Central – 2) (1981 – 1987) 250
48. Shooting the Messenger (1997) 255
49. The Indian Among the Cowboys (1992) 261
50. Ode to Fianna Fáil (1948) 265
51. Death on the Canvass – 3 (1948) 270
52. Safety in Number (One)s (1977) 273
53. Browned-Off Bertie (2007) 278
54. The Mole at the Polls (1973) 286
55. The Dancing PDs (2007) 290

For Peter and Charlotte Coleman

1

Rumble in Ranelagh
1997–2007

PROLOGUE

The struggle between the PDs' Michael McDowell and the Greens' John Gormley to win and retain a seat in leafy Dublin South-East, arguably the most prosperous constituency in the state (see Chapter 7), has been one of the most absorbing personal battles of the past decade in Irish politics.

It covered three general elections and entailed close calls, days of counting, rows, name-calling and the elevation of both men at different times to both the cabinet and leadership of their respective parties. Both can point to enormous achievements in the political world. But by the summer of 2007, only one of them would still be in politics.

THE DRAMA

Act 1 – The 1997 General Election
McDowell had been a national figure in Irish politics for over a decade by the time of the 1997 election. One of the four founding members of the PDs, he had first won a seat in 1987, losing it two

years later but regaining it in the 1992 general election. Extremely bright and certainly not lacking in confidence, McDowell was a formidable politician and the intellectual powerhouse of the PDs, although his abrasive – some would say arrogant – style brought many detractors.

In contrast, Gormley, although he had been Lord Mayor of Dublin, had a much lower profile. While McDowell and the PDs had big plans to get into government with Fianna Fáil, Gormley was simply aiming to join fellow Green TD Trevor Sargent in the Dáil. He was helped in this task by a disastrous campaign from the PDs which saw the party attract controversy over policies relating to single mothers and the reduction of the number of public servants.

McDowell's role, if any, in drawing up the party manifesto is unclear, but he certainly played a more low-key role in the PDs' national campaign than might have been expected. A decision had been taken by the election strategy committee to keep McDowell off the airwaves. 'We wanted a calm campaign and didn't want anybody rocking the boat, so we tried to keep him off the air as much as possible,' one strategist admitted to Stephen Collins in his definitive book on the PDs: *Breaking the Mould: How the PDs changed Irish Politics*. When the votes came in the day after the election, the PDs seemed to be in meltdown – at one point it looked like they would only have one TD. However, by late in the day, four seats had been secured. Michael McDowell was not one of those four – he was still locked in a battle with Gormley in a see-saw struggle for the fourth and final seat in Dublin South-East.

Just 27 votes lay between the two men when the votes were counted. And after seven days of counting, checking, rechecking, tagging and retagging the ballot papers, the seat remained unfilled. A magnifying glass, of the type that had first made its appearance

1 – Rumble in Ranelagh

THE RUMBLE IN RANELAGH

at a count in Dublin North-East in 1965 (see Chapter 13), was used to assess whether a ballot paper was properly perforated (the Americans clearly didn't invent the hanging chad as evidenced in the infamous Bush versus Gore 2000 US presidential election). During the seven agonising days, the two lawyer-laden sides – there were six senior counsel on the PDs' side and three on behalf of the Greens – checked the validity of all 36,761 votes cast. Of those, 336 were found to be in dispute. Examples of disputed papers included one where a voter had quite properly corrected his vote, but put his initials beside the change to 'confirm' its validity. One vote bore the words 'close Sellafield', while another had 'less fumes for cyclists' on it.

Of those 336 disputed votes, 158 were found to be valid. The two teams had been able to agree on all but around 30 of the 336 papers – the returning officer made the call on those. Both candidates required full details of the movement of all the relevant votes to be set out on paper and when that took longer than the expected two hours, the count was adjourned for another day. On the following day – the eighth – Gormley was deemed to be elected, having held onto his lead of just 27 votes.

Gormley paid tribute to McDowell, stating that while he 'disagreed profoundly with Michael on many political matters, I also regarded him as one of the most capable deputies in Dáil Éireann'. It seemed like the end of a short-lived rivalry. McDowell was devastated by the loss. The disastrous party manifesto rankled deeply and he was angered at how the campaign had been run and by what he believed was party policy to keep him off the airwaves during the campaign. McDowell quit the party a few months later.

Act II – The 2002 General Election
By the 2002 general election, though, McDowell was back and not just as a candidate, but as president of the PDs. He had been at the cabinet table since the middle of 1999, having been given the plum job of attorney general at the behest of Mary Harney. And, despite his previous protests to the contrary, it was of little surprise when it was announced that he would contest the upcoming election.

This time there was good news for both Gormley and McDowell. Both men were elected on the fourth count, filling the first two seats. While Gormley and the Greens were chuffed with their six seats, McDowell had even more reason to be satisfied. His decision to climb a lamp-post in Ranelagh with a 'One-Party Government – NO thanks!' poster was regarded as a turning point in the campaign (see Chapter 12) that prevented Fianna Fáil winning an overall majority and helped secure eight seats for the PDs. His reward was his dream job – cabinet minister at the Department of Justice.

Act III – The 2007 General Election
Five years on and the competition between the two men was as fierce as ever – some heated Dáil exchanges since the last election in 2002 did little to smooth relations between them.

By the time of the 2007 election, McDowell had become Tánaiste and leader of the PDs. Gormley was chairman of a Green Party that was expected to do great things in the election, but polls in the run-up and during the election showed the party's support was slipping. The same polls showed the PDs seriously struggling.

A resurgent Fine Gael increased the pressure on both men. It had selected a new female candidate for the constituency, Lucinda

Creighton. Dublin South-East has always been prime Fine Gael territory and the hard-working Creighton had the look of somebody who simply would not be denied a seat. With an almost certain seat for Fianna Fáil, and with Labour's Ruairi Quinn unlikely to lose out, both men must have sensed that, once again, they were fighting for the one seat.

The tensions famously came to a head in what was quickly dubbed 'the rumble in Ranelagh' (or alternatively 'the tangle at the triangle'). In truth though it was more Punch and Judy than Ali and Foreman. McDowell was attempting to repeat his 2002 trick of climbing a lamp-post with a poster, this time with the words 'Left Wing Government – No thanks!'

But he ran into an ambush by an indignant John Gormley. He had apparently been eating in the Dáil restaurant and had picked up word that McDowell was planning a spectacular early in the afternoon.

McDowell, flanked by deputy leader Liz O'Donnell and election candidate Tom Morrissey, was only a couple of minutes into his attack on Labour and the Greens – and how Fine Gael would be a political walkover in government – when a heckling Gormley appeared in the middle of the scrum of journalists, virtually eye-ball to eye-ball with McDowell.

The Justice Minister tried a quick put-down asking: 'Is that Michael Foot or John Gormley there?' – a reference to the eccentric-looking British Labour leader of the early 1980s – but the Green was not going to be put off. He declared that he had a booklet from the PDs that contained misleading information about the Greens' policies, including a claim that the party was going to raise corporation tax. Jabbing the booklet towards McDowell, he declared: 'That's a lie. That is a lie. It's a lie. Withdraw it. It's a total lie. Admit that it's a lie and withdraw it.'

McDowell, sounding like one of the characters from Harry Enfield's 'scousers' comedy sketch, urged Gormley to 'calm down' but he was wasting his breath. 'I'm not taking any more nonsense from you anymore. If you think you can intimidate me . . .' Gormley said, adding that he was 'sick and tired of this, the smear, the negativity. That's all you can do. Where are your positive ideas? No positive ideas at all.'

At times it was pure pantomime: 'You're out of the picture', 'No, you're out of the picture'. 'You're losing it, John'. 'No, you're losing it'. But of all the words Gormley uttered, he kept coming back to the same one: 'no, no, no, no' – which he repeated on roughly 20 occasions, which was understandable enough given all the adrenalin. Gormley exchanged 'pleasantries' with a number of PD officials at which point McDowell pleaded: 'John, will you relax please.' 'I am relaxed,' replied Gormley. Presumably responding to heckles of 'bye-bye', Gormley retorted: 'It's bye-bye to the PDs at this stage. You are history,' before going on to declare that the next government would be Fine Gael, Labour and the Greens – which seemed to conflict with his party's stance that it was fighting the election on a stand-alone basis.

'That's a scary thought,' retorted McDowell, 'given your performance today, John.' Gormley's phone rang and McDowell couldn't resist an uppercut: 'They're just ringing to say "don't make a fool of yourself".' Gormley responded with a neat jab: 'You're the guy that's made a fool of himself in the last two weeks. You've gone completely ga-ga.' This was presumably a reference to the PDs' perceived indecision as to whether or not to pull out of government a week after the election had been called. The PDs ultimately drew back from bringing down the government over the issue of Taoiseach Bertie Ahern's personal finances (see Chapter 55).

It was frantic stuff. Right at the end of the confrontation, as the two heavyweights licked their wounds, the fresh newcomer Lucinda Creighton strode up the street, climbed up a ladder and placed a poster featuring McDowell on a different pole with the words: 'Don't Want Single-Party Government? Well Thanks to Him That's a Reality'.

Nine days later the two men were back in the RDS for another struggle for the final seat – Creighton was comfortably elected. There was no marathon this time, but the result was, yet again, tight enough – though not relative to 1997 – with McDowell losing by just over 300 votes.

After 20 years in public life, an emotional McDowell arrived at the count centre declaring his love for Ireland and announcing he was quitting politics. He stopped short of doing a Richard Nixon and saying: 'You won't have Michael McDowell to kick around anymore,' but after all the flak he had taken over the previous five years – some justified, some unwarranted – he must have been tempted.

EPILOGUE

Only two of the eight PD deputies survived the election – Mary Harney and Galway West's Noel Grealish – but the Greens had also flattered to deceive. Despite predictions of ten or more seats, the party scraped back with the same number of deputies – six. However, the tightness of the numbers in the Dáil meant that both parties were in the shake-up to form a government.

As McDowell contemplated life after the PDs and politics, Gormley had little time to savour his victory, being thrown in as one of the Greens' negotiating team in coalition talks with Fianna

Fáil. By the end of those talks – after a wobble or two – the Greens had agreed a programme for government with their old enemy Fianna Fáil, which was endorsed by a thumping 84 per cent of their members. To increase the irony, the PDs would also be at the cabinet table – something that surely couldn't have happened had Michael McDowell also survived in Dublin South-East. The constituency that apparently doesn't elect TDs, only ministers, had lost one minister but gained a new one, as Gormley became Minister for Environment in the new government. It's hard to know which was the bigger achievement: becoming the first Green Minister for the Environment in the State's history or finally seeing off Michael McDowell in Dublin South-East. But he probably couldn't have achieved the former without first doing the latter.

2

Now You Tree it, Now You Don't
1982

PROLOGUE

It was 1982, a year that will forever be remembered for the politics of GUBU. Charlie Haughey was back in government, but his grip on power was tenuous. He had failed to deliver an overall majority in the first general election of that year, despite the embarrassing collapse of the Fine Gael and Labour coalition government over the infamous 'VAT on children's shoes' budget in January.

At 81 seats, plus the virtually guaranteed vote of independent Fianna Fáil deputy Neil Blaney, Haughey was effectively just one seat short of a de-facto majority. He was desperate to secure that extra seat and, in order to do so, came up with an audacious and outrageous plan (some would say 'stroke') to offer the vacant EEC commissionership to Fine Gael's Dublin West deputy Dick Burke, who had previously served in the role. After much deliberation, Burke agreed to take this position. This precipitated a by-election in his constituency which Haughey hoped to win, thereby giving his government a working majority in the Dáil.

So far, so good. But if Haughey thought that the tricky part of the plan was getting Burke to face down opposition from within

Fine Gael and accept the offer of the commissionership, he was completely mistaken. Even aside from concerns within Fianna Fáil that the move would be perceived as 'stroke-pulling', further damaging the party's image, Dublin West was always going to be a really tough constituency for Fianna Fáil to win in a by-election. Fine Gael had an advantage over Fianna Fáil there, holding three seats.

The good news for the government was that it seemed to have the stronger candidate in 49-year-old widow Eileen Lemass. Like Haughey, Eileen had married one of Seán Lemass's children. Aside from the advantage of bearing the Lemass name, as a former TD she was considerably more experienced than Fine Gael's candidate, 40-year-old Liam Skelly, who was a political novice.

Fianna Fáil threw the kitchen sink – and the kitchen cabinet – at the by-election. According to *The Boss: Charles J Haughey in Government,* Joe Joyce and Peter Murtagh's quite brilliant book on Haughey, each minister was allocated sub-sections of the constituency for which they were to be held responsible. TDs were told not to go home until after polling day.

Even the government's economic policy was affected. A decision in the March budget to introduce a large increase in employees' PRSI from 4.75 per cent to 7.5 per cent of gross pay from the start of April was watered down by the introduction of a generous new tax allowance for those paying the higher PRSI rates. While this concession was not purely due to the by-election, Joyce and Murtagh argued that the atmosphere created by the impending poll certainly helped bring it about. The government also headed off a threatened rise in mortgage rates by offering building societies cheap loans and lower taxes. Increases in children's allowances, due in July, were brought forward to May.

The constituents of Dublin West heard more promises than in a Bertie Ahern Ard-Fheis speech. A new factory for Blanchardstown? Check. More community centres and nine new schools? No problemo. Almost IR£300,000 for a sports centre in Ballyfermot? Sure. A hugely expensive new road bypassing the traditional bottlenecks of Lucan, Leixlip, Maynooth and Kilcock? Consider it done. Environment Minister Ray Burke also cut the sod for a road bypassing Palmerstown, despite complaints that the contracts for the road hadn't yet been signed.

The standard government-sponsored publicity campaigns were also used in a rather timely fashion. For example, the day before the by-election Lemass and Haughey appeared in newspaper ads appealing to the voters to 'strengthen the government's hand'. In the same newspapers, the Department of Health advertised that those earning less than IR£9,500 a year were now entitled to free hospital services.

THE DRAMA

Despite all the above promises, the Dublin West by-election of 1982 will always be infamous for another reason – the response by Environment Minister Ray Burke to complaints to party canvassers from residents in Clonsilla about the state in which their estate had been left by the developers. They had not received the trees that had been promised.

Burke organised to have young trees brought in and planted the night before the poll, but it was to be a strictly short-term measure as Joyce and Murtagh outlined in *The Boss:* 'The trees were planted throughout the estate, presumably as a visual encouragement to support Fianna Fáil when residents came out to vote the next day. But the trees also illustrated the illusory nature of some political promises; the day after the poll, the people from whom they had been borrowed dug them up and took them away again.'

EPILOGUE

The story has gone down in the annals as the ultimate in cynical electioneering. Not that the people of Dublin West were fooled. The two strokes – offering the commissionership to Dick Burke and lending trees to a housing estate for a few days (not to mention all the by-election promises) – didn't work, as Liam Skelly took the seat for Fine Gael in the by-election. It was 'as you were' in the Dáil in terms of seat numbers.

Haughey's government fell later in the year on a Dáil vote and, in the meantime, Fianna Fáil had given away one of the plummest jobs in Irish politics. Furthermore, the 'trees story' gave their opponents a stick to beat them with for the next two decades.

3

Owen's Goal
2002

PROLOGUE

It was supposed to symbolise our new modern, wealthy and confident image. High-tech, shiny new voting machines would replace what Bertie Ahern once described as 'our silly aul system' of paper and pencil. It was the way of the future, its advocates said, dismissing the concerns of those who worried that much of what people loved about the old voting system – the tallymen, the long-drawn-out counts, the various dramas due to transferred votes, the sense of suspense – would be lost.

At that early stage, there were few concerns about the accuracy of e-voting and whether the system was open to tampering. It was just a matter of how and when – not if – the new system would be introduced. It was decided that in the May 2002 general election, three constituencies – Dublin North, Dublin West and Meath – would act as guinea pigs for electronic voting. Assuming it was successful, electronic voting would be used nationwide in all future elections.

On the day of the vote, everything ran smoothly, with voters adapting to the new system quite easily. There were a few teething problems but they were generally down to human error, e.g. at one polling station a perceived fault turned out to be the operator forgetting to turn the machine on! There were also a few reports of plugs – wait for it – not being correctly pushed in. However, when push came to shove, so to speak, everything seemed to go well. The new system also meant that for the first time, the public wouldn't have to wait until the following day to discover the outcome of the vote; it was announced that the result in the three constituencies would be known within a few short hours of the polls closing.

THE DRAMA

A few years on and nobody really remembers what happened in Dublin West or Meath (or even that electronic voting was used in those constituencies), but the announcement of the result in Dublin North is already regarded as a piece of Irish election history. The count for the two Dublin constituencies took place in the Citywest Hotel and, despite the wonders of modern technology, the results were (surprise, surprise) a couple of hours late coming in.

The problem for the candidates was, unlike the traditional pencil-and-paper system (where tallymen could study the votes as they were counted and get a strong idea of how the result was shaping up), they didn't have a clue how the vote was going. In the old system, the result of each count was announced separately, often giving those candidates who would fail to be elected time to come to terms with the fact that they might fall short before their actual elimination was announced. On that night, there would be no time for adjustment, no gentle letdowns.

At 2.30am, just minutes before the result was announced, the sitting Fine Gael TD in Dublin North, Nora Owen – a grandniece of Michael Collins and a former Minister for Justice – told reporters that she was 'confident' of holding her seat. 'I believe there's a seat for Fine Gael in Dublin North. The reaction we are getting at the doors does not make me believe Fianna Fáil has two seats in this constituency.'

However, as is so often the case in Irish elections, the famed 'reaction at the doors' proved a poor indicator of what was to happen.

Once the result became available, the returning officer for Dublin North wrote the four names of the successful candidates on a piece of paper, prior to making the announcement. Fianna Fail's Jim Glennon, a former rugby international and a huge man, was able to look over the returning officer's shoulder as he was writing down the names. But with only a partial view, Glennon genuinely thought he saw the name 'N Owen' and turned to the Fine Gael TD, telling her 'you're in'.

However, when the result was announced, Owen was certainly not 'in'. The four successful candidates were Green Party leader Trevor Sargent, Labour's Sean Ryan, Glennon and GV Wright (also of Fianna Fáil). In the first indication of the Fine Gael meltdown in the 2002 general election that nearly wiped out the party, Owen – who was still walking with a crutch after an accident some weeks earlier – trailed in seventh. A very honourable man, Glennon later apologised to Owen for what was an honest mistake. Although he thought he had seen 'N Owen', it had actually been 'J Glennon' that was written on the piece of paper. The two names look quite similar written down.

It shouldn't have come to that. Under the old system, the writing would have been on the wall for Owen once the first count was

3 – Owen's Goal

YOU LOSE

YOU LOSE

YOU LOSE

YOU LOSE

YOU LOSE

YOU LOSE

announced, steeling her for the eventual outcome, but with electronic voting there was no preparation for what was to come. After 19 years serving the constituency, the news that she was 'out' was delivered in one brutal moment. To make matters worse, the result was broken to her in front of waiting photographers. Owen was clearly unprepared for the shock, and the shattered-looking former deputy leader of Fine Gael was immediately comforted by Labour's Sean Ryan; the photograph of Ryan's sensitive response to a fellow politician's distress became one of the defining images of that general election. Owen described the experience as akin to being stabbed very quickly.

'It was a terrible night,' she later recalled. 'It was the most inhumane circumstance that I have ever experienced. It was sudden death. That photograph of Sean Ryan comforting me will forever be the photograph associated with electronic voting.'

Owen also explained that she wasn't actually crying at the time of the famous photograph. 'I just put my hand up to my eyes to avoid the 20 cameras that were flashing in front of me.' But she did admit to shedding a few tears privately afterwards.

She was extremely critical of the way the night had been handled. 'It was a very, very traumatic experience – not just for me, my family, my friends and supporters, but for John Fitzpatrick, the returning officer who called out the result on the night. There was no room available where we could be told the results beforehand. The whole thing was a disaster.'

There was widespread sympathy for Owen's plight and few disagreed with the assessment that 'there's a cruelty and suddenness about the new system. It has to be changed.'

EPILOGUE

And changed it certainly would be. Largely because of the reaction to Owen's plight, a decision was made that in future each individual count would be announced in a staggered manner. This would have a dual impact of maintaining some of the suspense of the old system and protecting candidates from the big-bang approach adopted in 2002.

However, with the benefit of hindsight, that decision had something of the straightening of deckchairs on the *Titanic* about it. Electronic voting, it soon emerged, had much bigger problems than a lack of 'humanity and dignity'. After concerns were continually raised about the system's reliability, the government established an independent commission on electronic voting. The commission concluded that the machines 'were not of sufficient quality to enable their use to be confidently recommended and that functional testing revealed programming errors.'

While the commission concluded that the 7,500 voting machines were usable – subject to modifications and further rigorous testing – it said the key software used to count the votes on centralised computers in the system should be replaced.

Despite the government's insistence that this simply involved 'very minor adjustments', the hugely negative impact on public confidence in electronic voting was unmistakable. After spending more than €50 million on the system (along with significant ongoing annual costs for storing the machines), it was a huge embarrassment for the government. With the government forced to abandon plans to use electronic voting in the 2004 local and European elections and, subsequently, the 2007 general election, the machines have not been used since the night that Nora Owen learned, in such a cruel fashion, that she would not be returning to the Dáil. With concerns in other countries about the absence of a verifiable paper trail with electronic voting, there is no guarantee they will ever be used again. We may be stuck with 'our silly aul' system' for some time. Nora Owen would no doubt wish that we had never strayed away from it.

4

Wrap the Red Flag 'Round Me
1985

PROLOGUE

Election stunts are a risky business. When they work, you're a genius. When they don't, you can be left looking just a bit silly. Despite the risks, political parties and candidates will never stop trying to come up with innovative ways of stealing a march on their rivals and landing a headline in that evening's TV news or the following day's newspapers. Dignity just doesn't come into it.

So if that means donning a hard hat, riding in a donkey-and-cart or attempting to shoot a ball into an empty net and missing *à la* Diana Ross at the opening of the World Cup in the US in 1994, then so be it. Back in June 1985, Labour certainly needed something to give their local elections campaign a lift. The party had been in government with Fine Gael since late 1982, and it was clear that winning that election had proved to be a mixed blessing.

It was an awful time to be in government. The country was in the teeth of its worst recession since the grim days of the 1950s. Fine Gael and Labour didn't seem to have any answers to the problems that were ravaging the economy. A general election was still around two years away, but already an election defeat seemed inevitable.

THE DRAMA

Fergus Finlay, Labour's deputy government press secretary, came up with what seemed like a wonderfully imaginative idea of inviting the media out to the Weston Aerodrome in West Dublin to watch an aeroplane swoop down, pick up a large banner with a giant 'LABOUR' on it and 'soar off into the sky over Dublin'. Unfortunately, even though it was summertime the launch coincided with the wettest day of the year. In his excellent autobiography, *Snakes & Ladders*, Finlay hilariously recounts how it all went horribly wrong. 'When we got to the aerodrome, where our plane was waiting, the banner lay out in the grass, absolutely sodden and several times its normal weight. We had to carry it into a hangar to dry, and Dick [Spring, party leader] passed the time by posing for photographs, peering out through some of the letters with his colleagues. The photograph that appeared the next day showed Dick and Bernie Malone peering out through the letters "BO"!'

However, as Finlay recalls, worse was to come. 'The banner was eventually spread out on the ground, to be picked up by the aeroplane's tail hook. Once, twice, three times the plane swooped in, and each time it missed the banner. The cameras whirred, and the smiles on the politicians' faces grew more fixed and desperate.'

Think it couldn't get any worse? Think again. 'At the fourth attempt, the plane finally engaged the once-again sodden banner, and lifted off into the air, with "LABOUR" hanging straight down beneath it, instead of fluttering behind it. We all heard the plane cough and splutter as it tried to rise. Suddenly the pilot released the banner – he had to, otherwise its weight would have forced the plane into a stall. Our once-proud banner drifted slowly to earth, and ended up on wasteground near one of the Ballymun

Towers.'

EPILOGUE

The incident summed up the bad luck that government endured – if they'd had ducks, they would have drowned. But fair play to Finlay for telling the story against himself in his book. He wrote that for years after, every time he thought he had a bright idea for a stunt, one of his colleagues – quite often it was Dick Spring – would remind him of what happened that day. 'Not that I need reminding – I still have a video of the footage that *Today Tonight* [RTÉ's flagship current affairs programme of the era] lovingly took of the whole episode, and used as the centrepiece of their coverage of us during those elections. I fancy that when I arrive in hell, the devil will have that video to show me,' he wrote.

However, Finlay and Labour undoubtedly learned the lessons of that day and those painful four years in government. Although the government duly lost the general election of 1987, five years later Labour was back in government after the so-called Spring Tide secured the party its best ever election results when it increased its Dáil seats from 15 to 33.

5

In the Shadow of the Gunmen
1922

PROLOGUE

June 1922 and Ireland was about to enter the most traumatic year of its already troubled history. Tragically, the outbreak of the Civil War was only days away. Sinn Féin was split over the Treaty, which the delegation led by Arthur Griffith and Michael Collins had signed the previous winter. After a passionate debate, the second Dáil passed the Treaty by a small majority – 64 votes to 57. At that point de Valera, who strongly opposed the Treaty, resigned as president of the Dáil and was replaced by Griffith.

Griffith and Collins were determined to hold an election or referendum to allow the people to give their say on the Treaty. However, in order to prevent open competition between the two wings of Sinn Féin in the election, and in a vain attempt to head off a civil war and to ensure the election would not be interrupted by the IRA, the 'Collins-de Valera Pact' of 20 May was agreed, much to the chagrin of Griffiths and a watching Winston Churchill.

This involved each side nominating only as many candidates in each constituency as it had TDs in the second Dáil, ensuring, in theory, that the pro- and anti-Treaty factions would be returned in their existing strengths. A government would then be formed, made up of five pro-Treaty and four anti-Treaty ministers. With the pact in place, the contest threatened to be a re-run of the 1921 election when every constituency in the area, known the following year as the Free State, returned candidates unopposed (124 Sinn Féin candidates and four Unionists from Dublin University – see Chapter 30).

Although there was a clause in the pact acknowledging the right of other interests to stand, it was clear to Sinn Féin that with the STV-PR system being used, the pact could be undermined by non-Sinn Féin candidates entering the race.

THE DRAMA

It was the kind of general election that would make all future elections look dull, but not necessarily for the right reasons. Non-Sinn Féin candidates faced serious intimidation, no doubt a factor in the uncontested nature of eight of the 28 constituencies. Michael Gallagher points out in his excellent work, *Irish Elections 1922–44*, that with just 1.4 candidates per seat, the ratio of candidates to seats was lower than it has ever been since.

However, a number of non-Sinn Féin candidates did bravely contest the election, most notably Labour and the Farmers' Party. There were also former Home Rulers and various independents who put their names forward. All of these groups were in favour of the Treaty. The kind of courage that was required to stand in that election is best demonstrated by a Labour candidate in Tipperary, Dan Morrissey, who would go on to become a Fine Gael Minister. He was ordered by the IRA not to stand, but he secretly left his Nenagh home the night before nominations closed to make his way to Thurles.

Stephen Collins tells the story in his book *People, Politics and Power – From O'Connell to Ahern*: 'He got through the crowds outside the courthouse without being recognised and managed to hand in his nomination papers. Word spread quickly and when he came back out into the square, he was surrounded by hostile republicans. Ernie O'Malley, one of the ideologues of the IRA, took out a revolver, put it to Morrissey's head and told him to go back inside and withdraw his nomination. Although he feared he was going to be killed, Morrissey refused. At that moment one of the best-known IRA men in the country, Dan Breen, stepped forward, put a gun to O'Malley's head and told him that he would die if he shot Morrissey. O'Malley quickly put his gun down. Although Breen was on the republican side and had fought with O'Malley, he was from the same parish as Morrissey and they had distant ties of kinship. That counted for more than ideology for Breen, who was the only candidate in the election standing for both the pro- and anti-Treaty sides. Shots were subsequently fired into Morrissey's house during the campaign, but he had the satisfaction of being elected to the Dáil.'

Just to demonstrate how confused the political situation was, Stephen Collins writes that the same Dan Breen – who was standing for election in the Waterford-Tipperary constituency – was allegedly involved in intimidating a Farmers' Party candidate, who was subsequently shot and wounded and withdrew from the contest. Similar incidents of intimidation occurred across the country, prompting candidates to withdraw from the contest. 'One independent, Darrell Figgis, had to endure the indignity of having his beard shaved off in public by Republicans who wanted him to withdraw. He got his revenge by topping the poll in Dublin County,' Collins wrote.

There were enough candidates like Morrissey and Figgis to ensure that the Collins-de Valera pact was not successful. Tipperary is a good example of this. The seven-seater was supposed to have been divided four–three in favour of the Treaty side. However, the actual result was three pro-Treaty, two anti-Treaty, one Labour and one Farmers' Party.

The count took almost a week to complete. When the result came in, it showed a clear victory for the pro-Treatyites. The anti-Treaty candidates won just 20 per cent of the vote and 19 seats, compared to 41 seats for pro-Treaty Sinn Féin candidates. The non-Sinn Féin candidates performed extraordinarily well given the circumstances, taking a combined 40 per cent of the vote.

Labour won 21.3 per cent of the vote – a performance it has never repeated since – and all but one of its candidates were elected (the unlucky Labour man finished just eight votes short of a quota, according to Michael Gallagher). The Farmers' Party also won a seat in all but one of the constituencies it contested. Many high-profile names on the anti-Treaty side lost out, including Pádraig Pearse's mother Margaret, Kathleen Clarke (wife of another 1916 leader Tom Clarke), Countess Markievicz and Erskine Childers (who got just 512 votes in Kildare–Wicklow).

EPILOGUE

Republicans have always maintained that the result could not be taken as an endorsement of the Treaty, but it is difficult to avoid the conclusion that the general election of 1922, imperfect and all as it was, was just that. The turnout was low but that was partly accounted for by the poor state of the electoral register (something that would still be a problem in elections 85 years later!). Sadly, the relatively decisive result in the election was not the end of the divisions in the national movement; the bloody and brutal Civil War began a few days after the votes were counted. However, this election was key to ensuring that democracy put down firm roots in the newly-independent State. The primacy of the ballot box, rather than the gun, was asserted at a time when nobody could have taken this for granted. As Michael Gallagher points out, the presence of so many non-Sinn Féin candidates, despite the inherent dangers, made the election 'a genuine test of the people's will'.

He wrote that the 'election marked a contrast between two groups with very different views on the place of politics. One saw Irish society in essentially monist terms, as innately conflict-free. It wanted any differences of opinion to be resolved within the framework of the all-encompassing "national movement" and was suspicious of the very idea of political parties because the concept implied a fragmentation of the Irish people into different sections with different interests. The other took a more pluralist view, and saw the political process as existing in order to allow the peaceful resolution of conflicts that inevitably existed within Irish society.' The second view prevailed in the election, helping to establish 'the new Irish state as a twentieth-century liberal democracy', Gallagher concludes.

The election was effectively the first in which the STV-PR system was used, and voters took to it like ducks to water. Despite its complexity, only 3 per cent of votes were spoiled. Moreover, as Gallagher notes, voters clearly grasped the power STV gave them to differentiate between candidates of a particular party. Gallagher highlights the example of the seven-seat Galway constituency where the final seat came down to a battle between two anti-Treaty candidates – Frank Fahy and Liam Mellows. The latter, who was the leader of the 1916 Rising in the county, was seen as one of the most uncompromising of the republicans, while Fahy had made speeches 'in favour of the restoration of order and goodwill' to quote the *Connacht Tribune*. Transfers from pro-Treaty and Labour candidates enabled Fahy to overtake Mellows and get elected, despite trailing him by more than 500 votes on the first count.

It was an instrument that voters would use many times over the following eight decades.

6

The Dullest Election
1961

PROLOGUE

The October 1961 general election came at a crucial time in Ireland's development. After the grimness of the 1950s, the country was just starting to feel the early positive impact of a major change in government policy due to the Seán Lemass and Ken Whitaker-inspired Programme for Economic Expansion. Emigration was starting to fall, Ireland had applied for membership of the EEC on 31 July and Telefís Éireann was about to begin broadcasting at the end of the year.

Just as the election campaign was beginning, 150 Irish soldiers on UN duty in the Congo, Africa, in the Katagan area were attacked by a large force of the Katangese Gendarmerie at Jadotville and, after courageous resistance, were taken into captivity, where they were held until their release five weeks later. There was a serious strike in the ESB that prompted Lemass to recall the Dáil in September to enact special legislation to deal with a threatened breakdown of the power supply. This provoked huge opposition from the unions. All three of the leading political parties had new leaders – Lemass, who would go on to be widely regarded as the country's best ever Taoiseach, had finally succeeded de Valera as leader of Fianna Fáil and Taoiseach a couple of years earlier; Fine Gael was now led by James Dillon, regarded as one of Irish politics' greatest orators, and Labour had a new, young, dynamic head in Brendan Corish. Throw in the presence of Noel Browne as head of the National Progressive Democrats, and all the ingredients seemed to be there for a rollicking general election.

THE DRAMA

Eh . . . well . . . em . . . there wasn't any really. Lemass biographer John Horgan wrote in *Seán Lemass – the Enigmatic Patriot* that there was, 'a general air of lassitude' about the election. Despite the richness of the potential topics on which the main parties could have fought the election, the big issue was – wait for it – how Irish should be taught in schools. Just a couple of days before the campaign kicked off, Fine Gael had proposed that the compulsory teaching of infants through Irish in national schools should be stopped outside the Gaeltacht areas. It also wanted to make Irish an optional subject for the Leaving Certificate – ending the system whereby if a student failed Irish, he or she failed the Leaving Cert exams. Fine Gael also called for a revision of the Irish requirement for public sector appointments and a repeal of the obligation to qualify in Irish for certain professional qualifications.

The proposal received editorial backing from *The Irish Times* ('Sense at Last' was the headline) but was roundly attacked by Fianna Fáil, with one parliamentary secretary (the equivalent of a junior minister today) accusing Fine Gael of 'national treachery'. Declan Costello, one of the leading figures in Fine Gael at the time, responded that it was not treachery to do away with bumptious hypocrisy.

The more general charge from Fianna Fáil was that Fine Gael

had no appreciation of the importance of the national language. Cabinet minister Neil Blaney described it as a 'cheap trick' to confuse the electorate and warned that it would be 'a sad day if any native government attempted to do what centuries of oppression had failed to do.' Contrary to what Blaney said, and sadly for the Irish language, 'centuries of oppression' had widely succeeded in having a detrimental effect on the use of the language.

James Dillon replied that the current system was simply wrong and that compulsion was promoting opposition to, and dislike of, the language. The Gaeltacht was dwindling and the Irish language had lost its popularity with the young. 'A new departure is urgently needed if we are to stop the rot and revive the old enthusiasm which launched the Gaelic League and united all the sections of our people in the cause of the Irish revival more than 50 years ago,' Dillon said, adding that young people should not be denied the right to earn their living and get their education simply because they were not linguistically gifted in any particular language. One of those accused of not being linguistically gifted, interestingly enough, was Seán Lemass whom Fine Gael regularly lambasted for his inability to speak the national *teanga*. As Horgan wrote, Dillon once said that Lemass couldn't 'bid a dog good day in Irish'. However, this didn't stop Lemass strongly attacking the Fine Gael proposal.

In some ways, the whole subject was an interesting and worthwhile debate which, as Horgan noted, offered some relief from the earnest agenda set by Lemass. However, whether it warranted being such a central issue in a general-election campaign in a country that was just emerging from a decade of deep depression with high unemployment and huge emigration rates, is doubtful. Over four decades later, when another Fine Gael leader, Enda Kenny, raised the issue of compulsory Irish, it did prompt a debate but it never threatened to become a major point of division in the ensuing general election. There were simply too many more important issues. There was some debate on the economy in 1961, but it was hardly inspiring. Fianna Fáil reminded voters of the dire state of the economy the last time a Fine Gael-led coalition had power between 1954 and 1957. With a wonderful sense of overstatement, Lemass warned that there were increasing doubts as to whether the country would survive a third depression caused by a coalition government.

To be fair to all involved, the election may have been overshadowed by the fallout from events in the Congo. Lemass's government had just sorted out the ESB strike – allowing him to announce the election a day later – when he was immediately confronted by another crisis that could have forced a postponement. Another Lemass biographer, Brian Farrell, wrote, ' . . . on the same night the Minister for Defence reported a rumoured massacre of 150 troops in the Congo. The dilemma was intensified by the belief that most casualties came from the Athlone garrison – the town chosen by Lemass to begin his campaign. In the event the story proved unfounded. However, none of this provided a helpful background to Fianna Fáil's first general election without de Valera.'

It certainly didn't. The dissolution of the Dáil didn't even make the front page of the *Irish Press*, of all papers, because of events in the Congo. Lemass actually cancelled election meetings on the first weekend of the campaign because of the need to deal with the issue, and throughout the election he addressed only 15 meetings. Although the reports of the massacre were untrue, the Irish troops were in captivity for the duration of the election campaign. Lemass actually felt the need to explain why it was still important and in the national interest to proceed with the general election in the circumstances. The departure of de Valera may also have been a factor in the dullness of the election, with John Horgan noting that 'extreme caution was the order of the day, as the party and its leader tiptoed into the post-de Valera era with considerable apprehension'.

EPILOGUE

The election may have been a bore, but the result certainly was not. There were widespread predictions of a new election after no side won a majority. As expected, after its stunning election triumph of four years earlier, Fianna Fáil lost seats – eight in total – but the losses were not as serious as the party had feared, although it was three short of an overall majority. Fine Gael and Labour both gained seats – seven and three respectively – but their total of 63 seats was still seven behind Fianna Fáil, and Labour was ruling out the idea of coalition after the hammering it had taken in 1957 when coming out of government. Despite his party not having the votes to re-elect him Taoiseach, Lemass took a tough line and did no deals with independents, essentially inviting them to support his nomination or face the uncertainty of another election. 'I have not asked any deputy in this House, outside the members of my own party, to support the motion, either by their vote or by their abstention,' Lemass told the Dáil. 'If I should be elected Taoiseach, it would be my intention to implement the programme of my party in all respects.' He was and he did and although there were some moments of crisis, Lemass successfully managed his minority government for the next three and a half years until he called an election in April 1965. After the dullness of the campaign in 1961, it was perhaps no surprise that there was no rush to have another election.

7

Three Hail Marys
1977 – 1987

PROLOGUE

There are few higher-profile constituencies than Dublin South-East. Some of that is undoubtedly down to the fact that it is home to the 'Dublin 4 set' – the phrase memorably coined by the late *Irish Times* journalist John Healy as a pejorative description of the political constituency of Dublin South-East. Actually, there is a lot more to Dublin South-East than affluent Dublin 4 – there is also affluent Dublin 6 and Dublin 8! In reality though, the constituency also includes large working-class areas. As long-time Dublin South-East TD Ruairi Quinn once put it, the constituency extends 'all the way from skid row to embassy row' and later wrote: 'From Ailesbury Road in the heart of Dublin 4 to the Iveagh Hostel close to St Patrick's cathedral, all humankind are encompassed representing and comprising the best and the worst of all Ireland's successes and its failures.' There can be no arguing with the constituency's influence on national politics. As Ruairi Quinn and Ross Higgins note in their book, *A History of Dublin South-East Constituency*, it has provided the state with two Taoisigh, three Tánaiste, two Ministers for Finance, six party leaders (John Gormley being the most recent) and three presidents. A female voter summed up the views of many in the constituency when she commented to a Labour party activist in Dublin South-East: 'Oh, we don't elect TDs here; we elect ministers.'

THE DRAMA

That voter is right, but not completely. Take the case of the three highest-profile female politicians since the foundation of the State – the three Marys: Robinson, McAleese and Harney. All have enjoyed phenomenonly successful political careers. Robinson was the State's first female president, handing Fianna Fáil its first ever defeat in a presidential election in the process of getting to the Áras. She was succeeded by McAleese, who fought off Albert Reynolds to win the Fianna Fáil nomination and then came through a bruising contest to serve for two terms. Harney, meanwhile, has been one of the most respected politicians of the past thirty years. The first ever female leader of a major political party, a Tánaiste for nine years and a cabinet minister in the Departments of Enterprise, Trade and Employment and Health. Apart from being called Mary and enjoying enormous political success, the three women have something else in common – they were all rejected by the voters of Dublin South-East.

Technically, Mary Robinson didn't fail to win a seat in Dublin South-East – she contested the newly created Dublin Rathmines constituency in 1977. However, it comprised Harold's Cross, Rathgar, Ranelagh and Rathmines, the vast majority of which were previously, and subsequent to the 1977 election, part of Dublin South-East. The new Dublin Rathmines constituency was only created as part of Local Government Minister Jim Tully's infamous 'Tullymander' (see Chapter 32), which created a series of three-seaters in Dublin on the basis that Fine Gael and Labour would each get one seat, leaving Fianna Fáil with just one out of three – thereby supposedly guaranteeing the Fine Gael-Labour coalition's return to power. It backfired spectacularly as Fianna Fáil's vote surged and the party ended up winning two out of three in most Dublin constituencies. In that 1977 election, the Labour party leadership wanted Robinson, a well-respected barrister with a record of campaigning on women's rights, to run in Dublin Rathmines. Robinson formed two new branches – Neagh Road and Leinster Road – to make sure she had a fighting chance of selection. According to Quinn and Higgins, 'a row erupted when the constituency party voted 25–1 not to accept them as, according to party rules, branches had to be in existence for over six months to vote.' The matter was passed to Labour's Administrative Council, the party's national governing body, which 'came up with the novel solution of announcing that the party constitution in fact referred to lunar months and not calender ones!' As lunar months are shorter, the branches were thus deemed to be in existence for a sufficient length of time. Robinson was ultimately added to the ticket as one of two Labour candidates. However, although she polled reasonably well with around half a quota, the enormous strength of Fianna Fáil in that election consigned her to fourth place and she missed out on a seat.

In the same election, Mary Harney, then in her early twenties, contested the Dublin South-East constituency for Fianna Fáil. However, Harney fell well short of winning a seat. The strength of outgoing Foreign Affairs Minister and future Taoiseach Garret FitzGerald helped the coalition buck the national trend and take two out of three seats. A young Ruairi Quinn was elected for the first time and Fianna Fáil's Seán Moore was also returned. Harney, with a quarter of a quota, was well behind the other unsuccessful Fianna Fáil candidate Peter Gibson.

A decade later, it was Mary McAleese who failed to impress the voters of Dublin South-East. At the time McAleese was a well-known journalist, having presented RTÉ's then flagship current affairs programme *Today Tonight*. She was also Reid Professor of Criminal Law in Trinity College – a position once held by Mary Robinson. But McAleese secured just 29 per cent of a quota or 2,243 votes – ahead of running mate Eoin Ryan, but behind the other two names on the Fianna Fáil ticket and well short of the number required to take a seat from either the PDs' Michael McDowell or Labour's Ruairi Quinn. Outgoing Taoiseach Garret FitzGerald, unsurprisingly, topped the poll. Gerard Brady, who had topped the poll in Dublin Rathmines in 1977 when Mary Robinson had failed to be elected, comfortably took the Fianna Fáil seat.

EPILOGUE

In American Football, the term 'Hail Mary pass' is used when, in the dying seconds of the game, the quarterback, generally on a losing side, speculatively throws the ball long towards the end zone because there is no realistic possibility for any other play to work and there is an outside chance that by some fluke the pass will work out.

And to be fair to Robinson, Harney and McAleese, their respective parties were attempting the political version of the 'Hail Mary pass' by asking them to win a Dáil seat in the Dublin South-East area, given the level of opposition they faced. Robinson was up against an enormous Fianna Fáil vote nationally in 1977, while in the same election Harney was an unknown novice up against a formidable Fine Gael/Labour ticket. A decade later in 1987, despite the unpopularity of the outgoing Fine Gael/Labour government, McAleese's chances of winning a second seat for her party in the constituency – always a challenge for Fianna Fáil in Dublin South-East – were hampered by the presence of the newly formed Progressive Democrats and by her party's decision to run four candidates. However, despite their setbacks in leafy Dublin South-East, it worked out exceptionally well for all three. Robinson spent some time in the Seanad before shocking everybody by taking the presidency against all the odds in 1990. Harney also spent a few years in the upper house, having received a Taoiseach's nomination in 1977 from Jack Lynch, and was subsequently elected to the Dáil in Dublin South-West in 1982, where she remained as a TD for 20 years before boundary changes saw her switch to Dublin Mid-West in 2002. She was expelled from the Fianna Fáil parliamentary party in late 1985 after voting alongside Des O'Malley in favour of the Anglo-Irish Agreement, against her party line. Less than a month later, she formally resigned from the Fianna Fáil organisation and became a founding member of the PDs, where she has enjoyed a glittering political career. McAleese emerged from a decade-long political wilderness after her 1987 electoral setback, to come from nowhere to win the Fianna Fáil presidential nomination and then, weeks later, be elected president. It certainly turned out alright for the three Marys.

In the 2007 general election, meanwhile, the observation that Dublin South-East voters don't elect TDs, they elect ministers, was turned on its head when Minister for Justice Michael McDowell sensationally lost his seat (see Chapter 1). However, the constituency did secure a seat at cabinet in the form of John Gormley.

8

The Postman Knocked Once (Dublin Central – 1)

2007

PROLOGUE

Bertie Ahern has been a Minister for Finance, the State's second-longest serving Taoiseach, a president of the European Union and has turned down the job of president of the European Commission. But, despite his success on the national and international stage, he has never forgotten the old Tipp O'Neill adage that 'all politics is local'. He has utterly dominated his constituency of Dublin Central with the help of a powerful local organisation, dubbed the Drumcondra mafia. Even as Taoiseach, Ahern has never let his guard down in the constituency, regularly canvassing it at weekends – well outside election time – like a hopeful first-time contender.

Being a running mate of Ahern's was always a dubious privilege. The bad news was that first-preference votes were likely to be hoovered up by the main man, but by way of compensation some juicy morsels were likely to be tossed from the poll topper's table in the form of transfers, which could be enough to get the second Fianna Fáil candidate over the finishing line. Despite (or maybe because of) Ahern's undoubted ability to garner huge first-preference votes, his party has rarely had it easy in taking two seats in the constituency. For example, in 2002 – the election in which Fianna Fáil came within a few hundred votes of an overall majority – Ahern barely avoided the embarrassment of failing to bring in a running mate because of a poor spread of votes between the two Fianna Fáil candidates. Ahern got 1.6 quotas and over four times the votes of his running mate Dermot Fitzpatrick. The latter was eventually elected by just 79 votes, having secured the lowest first-preference vote of any successful candidate with 2,590. In 2007, the task of holding Fianna Fáil's two seats appeared even more difficult when three candidates were chosen on the ticket. Ahern was joined by Cyprian Brady and Mary Fitzpatrick. Brady had run Ahern's constituency office and had been his eyes and ears in Dublin Central for 20 years. He had been rewarded with a seat in the Seanad by the Taoiseach in 2002. Mary Fitzpatrick, meanwhile, was the daughter of outgoing TD Dermot Fitzpatrick. Given that Fianna Fáil's head office was insisting on the correct number of candidates in each constituency, it was widely expected that one of the two running mates would be dropped from the ticket in advance of polling day. However, this was the Taoiseach's backyard, where he called the shots, and, not surprisingly, that never happened. With Fianna Fáil struggling in the opinion polls nationally and facing apparently stiff competition locally in the form of Sinn Féin's Mary Lou McDonald and the Greens' Patricia McKenna, most commentators were predicting that Ahern would fail to deliver two seats in Dublin Central.

THE DRAMA

Fianna Fáil had a surprisingly good day nationally. The Taoiseach delivered his usual huge first-preference haul, 12,734 votes –

almost two quotas. Sinn Féin and the Greens struggled to deliver a vote on the day and, with Fianna Fáil's three candidates delivering 2.22 quotas overall, it was quickly apparent that Ahern would, after all, bring in a running mate. A casual observer of the first count result would have expected that to be Mary Fitzpatrick. After all, she had secured 1,725 first-preference votes – almost twice as many as Brady, who was lying in ninth place with just 939 votes (just 2.7 per cent of the total first-preference vote) after the first count. However, it was Brady who did best from the transfer of the Taoiseach's huge surplus (2,403 versus Fitzpatrick's 1,362), and by the second count he was ahead of Fitzpatrick by 255 votes. When the fifth vote was announced, he was still 169 votes clear and it was Fitzpatrick rather than Brady who was eliminated. Fitzpatrick's large transfer to him effectively guaranteed Brady the seat. His final vote tally, after he was elected on the eighth count, was 6,348 votes, but his first-preference vote of 939 was one of the lowest ever secured by an elected candidate, particularly in modern times. To put it into perspective, in 2002 former Tánaiste Dick Spring failed to win a seat having received 8,773 votes, over nine times the amount obtained by Brady. Sometimes it's good to be Bertie Ahern's running mate.

EPILOGUE

Only sometimes, mind you – and not if your name happens to be Mary Fitzpatrick. It didn't take long for the recriminations to start. They centred around the distribution of 30,000 letters to homes in the constituency, just hours before polling started, urging voters to vote number one Ahern, number two Brady and number three Fitzpatrick. The letter was signed by the Taoiseach and headlined in red with the words 'IMPORTANT NOTICE'. It asked the reader to 'support the party strategy' (also in red) in maximising support in Dublin Central by voting 'in this area' 1 Ahern, 2 Brady and 3 Fitzpatrick. Given that the letters were sent to every home in the constituency, it's not clear why the words 'in this area' were included.

Fitzpatrick and her team were furious at the decision by the Fianna Fáil constituency organisation to 'drop' (i.e. deliver) the letter throughout the constituency. In fact, they blamed this letter for her narrow defeat in the election and were outraged that the drop had been carried out throughout the constituency rather than just in Ahern or Brady's areas within the constituency. Fitzpatrick's anger was brilliantly captured by RTÉ radio's Ann-Marie Power, who was conducting a documentary on the contest between the three high-profile female politicians in Dublin Central, entitled *Patricia, Mary and Mary Lou too*. The documentary was broadcast within days of the election and listeners were left in little doubt as to what Fitzpatrick thought. She bluntly stated that she had been 'shafted' and 'sabotaged' by the local organisation.

'I never thought they were the Legion of Mary. I never thought they were going to do me any favours. I thought my insurance policy was that they needed a second seat, so I didn't think they would go out to completely undermine me and shaft me,' she told the programme.

Fitzpatrick was scathing about Brady's performance: 'He had 900 votes after 20 years supposedly of loyal service, working the constituency, blah, blah, blah, and all he could deliver was 900 first-preference votes.'

Not surprisingly, Ahern's team rejected any suggestions that Fitzpatrick had been shafted, noting that others had stood down to clear the way for Fitzpatrick to win the nomination at convention time. Asked about the by-now infamous letter from Bertie Ahern, the Taoiseach's team responded that Fitzpatrick had first contravened an agreement by dropping a leaflet in her ward asking for number 1 – something she had been asked not to do. 'Having then done it, she therefore effectively set in train a motion which she wasn't going to be able to stop,' one of Ahern's team told the documentary.

Fitzpatrick was dismissive of the suggestion that the letter was a response to something she had done. 'So they'd seen my canvass card for three weeks and then, all of a sudden, it was an issue? It's not an issue. That isn't why they did it. They did it because they wanted to hammer me.' She added that to try and 'pretend that they did that letter out of retaliation for a colour flier from me, that probably wasn't picked up because it looked like one of my canvass cards, I don't buy it. I don't accept it. And that doesn't explain why the [Dublin] Central [FF] newspaper that they put out earlier in the campaign made no mention of me; why the education colour leaflets that they put out throughout the constituency made no mention of me and why in any properties that they had 8' x 4' billboards in they couldn't accommodate any of my billboards . . . They didn't want me to get elected.'

Fitzpatrick, along with making some unflattering remarks about the Brady team's canvassing style, claimed the only way the local Fianna Fáil organisation could get Brady elected was to get her to deliver the Fianna Fáil vote on the Navan Road – her father's electoral base – adding: 'Without me, they wouldn't have had that vote and they know that.'

With 2007 likely to have been Bertie Ahern's last general election and Brady now the Taoiseach's clear heir-apparent, it should make for an interesting election in Dublin Central in 2011/2012.

9

I Deem the Candidate ... Nicked
1923 – 25

PROLOGUE

The fourth Dáil has the record for the most by-elections, with an extraordinary 21 new TDs elected in its four years (see Chapter 28), but the circumstances that caused two of these by-elections – in Mayo North and Laois–Offaly – were truly remarkable. TDs representing these two constituencies were disqualified from the Dáil after being sentenced to a prison term exceeding six months.

THE DRAMA

Act I
On 18 October 1923 – less than two months after he was elected to the Dáil as a Cumann na nGaedheal TD – Henry Coyle went to the proprietor of the Ormond Hotel in Dublin, a Patrick J O'Malley, and produced a cheque payable to himself for £450.

The cheque was signed in Irish and Coyle told O'Malley that the signature was that of his uncle, whom he described as one of the principal cattle dealers in Mayo. He asked O'Malley to 'oblige him' by endorsing the cheque and O'Malley, believing the story (not surprisingly, given that it was told to him by an upstanding member of Dáil Éireann), did so. However, when the cheque was cashed in the Bank of Ireland, it turned out to be forged. Coyle was arrested, though not until the following March, and was indicted to appear in front of the Dublin Commission Court on the charge of 'fraudulently' inducing O'Malley to endorse the cheque 'which purported to be a valid order for the payment of £450'.

The prosecuting counsel, a Mr Carrigan, said the case was important because of the amount involved and the position held by Coyle. Describing Coyle's actions as a 'scandalous fraud', Carrigan said Coyle had placed £100 in O'Malley's bank account, but £350 was still outstanding. After O'Malley gave his evidence, Coyle's counsel informed the court his client was withdrawing his plea of 'not guilty' and instead pleading guilty. His counsel suggested that Coyle should be given the opportunity to pay back the money.

The judge warned Coyle that this would be 'no palliation [excuse] of the actual offence'. And any possible palliative effect was firmly ended when no money was forthcoming by the following Monday. Coyle, addressing the court, said that when he had persuaded O'Malley to endorse the cheque he had no intention of defrauding him. He added that he was disappointed at the way the State had pressed the case, as his past service had not been taken into account.

However, in relation to 'past service', the prosecuting counsel told the court he had received a telegram from Glasgow police saying there was, at present, a warrant out against Coyle for defrauding a man of £500. The judge said, given the TD's 'most responsible position', the fact that he had pleaded guilty to securing money under false pretences and that the promise of money in recompense had not been forthcoming, he could not pass a smaller sentence than three years' penal servitude. Judge Samuels subsequently wrote to the Speaker of Dáil Éireann informing him of Coyle's conviction. Under Section 51 of the Electoral Act, Coyle was later disqualified from the Dáil, going from 'servant of the state' to 'guest of the nation'.

Act II
Just over a year after Coyle's sentencing, late on 22 April 1924, a civil guard, Sergeant Daniel Finucane, on patrol duty with two other guards, was passing a public house near Ballinagore, County Offaly, where he saw a light. Suspecting a breach of the licensing laws, he knocked on the door and, after some delay, was admitted. There was 'no non-bona fide travellers' on the premises, but he heard people going out the back of the building.

Finucane and his colleagues went through to the rear of the premises and when they got into a field near the house, they heard shouts of 'Halt!' They saw seven men ahead of them, three of whom approached Finucane and told him to put up his hands. He declined to do so and told the men he had no arms on him. At this point, Sean McGuinness, who was a Republican TD for Laois–Offaly, struck Finucane on the face and, according to the sergeant's later evidence in court, said: 'You might call yourself a lucky man that you were not shot when told to put up your hands.' The three men were armed with revolvers, Finucane said, also claiming that McGuinness told him that 'if you report this to the authorities, I will paint the road red with your blood'. Finucane rather bravely told the men that he would be reporting it in the morning and the men left.

Five days later at another public house, this time in Doris, near Nenagh, McGuinness was approached by peace officer Lawrence

9 – I Deem the Candidate . . . Nicked

O'Neill and, on being asked his name, produced a revolver. O'Neill later testified that McGuinness threatened to blow the officer's brains out. He said he did not know McGuinness at the time, but identified him a couple of months later at Portarlington Station. At the Central Criminal Court on 29 October 1925, McGuinness was found guilty of assaulting, resisting and wilfully obstructing Sergeant Finucane in the execution of his duty and of assaulting peace officer Lawrence O'Neill at the pub in Doris.

He was sentenced to 18 months' imprisonment with hard labour in each case, with the sentences to run concurrently. A further charge of being in unlawful possession of a revolver was dropped.

Addressing the jury, McGuinness – who as an anti-Treaty Republican hadn't taken his seat in the Dáil – said that as a soldier of the Irish Republic and an elected representative of that Republic, he denied the right of the court to try him. Any action he had taken, he said, was in self-defence. Certain people may wish to brand him as a criminal but he referred those who sought to do so to his constituents. McGuinness further alleged 'inhuman treatment' in Mountjoy Prison. The principal warder of the prison, who also took the stand, denied this. In sentencing McGuinness, Justice O'Shaughnessy said that as he was an elected representative of the Dáil, he (the judge) was bound to notify the speaker of the Dáil of his conviction and he would do so.

McGuinness was duly disqualified from the Dáil he did not recognise on 28 November 1925.

EPILOGUE

To paraphrase Oscar Wilde, losing one TD to prison was unfortunate; losing two was downright careless. The two by-elections saw Cumann na nGaedheal and the Republicans swap seats. In November 1924, on the same day that Seán Lemass won a seat in a by-election in Dublin South, the Republicans' John Madden made it a double victory by surprisingly winning the by-election in Mayo North caused by Coyle's disqualification. However, in February 1926, Cumann na nGaedheal turned the tables by taking the seat in the Laois–Offaly by-election caused by the disqualification of McGuinness.

10

The Ultimate Poll Topper
1923 – 48

PROLOGUE

General Richard Mulcahy was one of the most controversial politicians of the early decades of the new State. To his supporters, he was the man who fought for his country and, when independence was won, took responsibility for what had to be done to protect the Free State from forces unwilling to accept the Treaty which had been endorsed by the people. To his detractors, he was commander-in-chief of the Free State army and Minister of Defence in a government responsible for the ruthless execution of key anti-Treaty figures who had been heroes in the War of Independence.

Although Mulcahy was criticised within his own party by the likes of Kevin O'Higgins for not being even tougher with irregulars at this time, there is no question that his role in the Civil War, and his identification by the public as being intimately connected with the executions, denied him a place in the popular pantheon of Irish heroes.

However, his service to the State is beyond doubt. Waterford-born Mulcahy fought in 1916 and as the organisational and planning brain behind Michael Collins, he was a vital figure in directing the War of Independence. He became Minister for

Defence in the post-Treaty Dáil, but when the Civil War broke out he returned to the army as chief of staff and then commander-in-chief when Collins was killed. From 17 November 1922 to 2 May 1923, the government executed 77 people as it opted for a draconian response to IRA terror. Opinions differ as to whether these methods shortened the Civil War, saving innocent lives in the process, or simply stiffened the resolve of the anti-Treatyites to continue.

However, after the assassination of Sean Hales in December 1922, there were no further attempts on the lives of Dáil deputies during this time. Hales and the Leas Ceann Comhairle of the Dáil, Pádraic Ó Máille, were shot in Dublin on their way to the Dáil on the day the new Free State constitution was enacted. Hales was killed, while Ó Máille was wounded. A number of TDs fled Dublin in fear of their lives after the shooting, but William T Cosgrave, anxious to ensure democracy would not be compromised, ordered the secret service to bring the deputies back to Dublin.

In reprisal for the shooting of Hales and Ó Máille, the cabinet ordered the execution of four imprisoned high-profile IRA leaders: Rory O'Connor, Liam Mellows, Richard Barrett and Joe McKelvey – one from each of the four provinces. The decision to execute these four leaders was extremely controversial and was condemned by Labour and other opposition TDs. However, Cosgrave was unmoved, arguing that IRA terror had to be crushed and met with terror.

When the Civil War ended in May 1923, Cosgrave, who became President of the Executive Council when the Free State formally came into existence in December 1922, called a general election for August – the country's first relatively normal election since 1910. No doubt the severe economic depression was a major factor, but it was far from the expected landslide for Cumann na nGaedheal, with the party winning 39 per cent of the vote and 63 seats – a gain of just five instead of the predicted 20-plus advances commentators were predicting. Labour, beset by bitter internal wrangles in the trade union movement, had a disastrous election, with its share of the vote falling from 21 per cent to 12 per cent.

Sinn Féin proved surprisingly resilient, despite most of its leaders, including de Valera, being in jail. It won 27.6 per cent of the vote and 44 seats, much higher than forecast. Although the party's abstentionist policy precluded it from taking its seats in the Dáil, J.J. Lee wrote in *Ireland 1912–1985 – Politics and Society* that 'the result gave de Valera a chance to escape from the grip of the gunmen'.

THE DRAMA

While his party may not have been living up to expectations, the general election was a personal triumph for Mulcahy. In his constituency of Dublin City North, he won an extraordinary 22,205 first-preference votes – the highest ever received in a Dáil election before or since – equating to 40 per cent of the valid poll. General Mulcahy's son, Risteard, in his book *Richard Mulcahy, A Family Memorial*, wrote that this 'whopping vote' was 'surely a powerful endorsement by the electorate of the Clontarf constituency of his leadership of the army during the Civil War.' His biographer, Maryann Gialenella Valiulis, also wrote that Mulcahy can only have taken this huge vote 'as an endorsement of his policy'.

EPILOGUE

Despite this massive vote, Mulcahy became somewhat isolated in Cumann na nGaedheal. Unlike many of his cabinet colleagues, he viewed the Treaty as merely a stepping stone to a united, Irish-speaking Ireland. As Minister for Defence, Mulcahy also had the very tricky job of reducing army numbers, which had become bloated in size during the Civil War.

He advocated an army that was politically impartial and ready to serve, even under a de Valera government. In responsibly attempting to handle the many problems in the army – not least the different factions that existed there – in a careful and non-confrontational manner, he found himself bitterly criticised by his cabinet colleagues and he was forced out (resigning, before he was pushed, over the sacking of the army council in the wake of the army mutiny of 1924).

Despite Mulcahy being lambasted by Kevin O'Higgins as a traitor to democracy, J.J. Lee and others have noted that Mulcahy's restrained response to his dismissal – in Lee's words he was the 'one man who might have roused sufficient military support to pose a real threat to the government' was crucial to the infant state. 'It was probably only Mulcahy's decision – the sign not of a weak man, but of a committed democrat – to accept his humiliation that forestalled a really serious crisis,' wrote Lee.

Mulcahy was brought back from the cold by Cosgrave in 1927, becoming Minister for Local Government and Health. He became leader of Fine Gael in 1944 and organised the first inter-party government of 1948. But true to form, he stood aside to allow John A. Costello become Taoiseach when it became clear Clann na Poblachta could not stomach being led in government by the commander of the Free State forces during the Civil War. Mulcahy instead became Minister for Education, a position he also filled in the second inter-party government of 1954–57.

Mulcahy may sit in first place in the general-election league table of vote-getters (Cecil Lavery did get more votes, 43,671, in a by-election in Dublin County, contested by just two candidates in 1935), but that did not protect him from the fickle nature of voters' preferences. In the elections of 1937 and 1943, the country's highest ever vote-winner in a general election lost his seat, although each time he did win it back at the next general election. In 1944 he moved constituency to Tipperary.

The results of the 1923, 1937 and 1943 general elections seem to be a metaphor for the amazing highs and lows that Mulcahy encountered in his political life. Although Mulcahy was overshadowed by many of his peers, John A Costello summed up the views of many when he said: 'He served his country well, but it was not appreciated. I personally have never come across any man who was so selfless in public or national affairs.'

11

Consulting the Stars
1977

PROLOGUE

Nowadays every general-election campaign is dominated by opinion polls. In the 2007 general election, not only were there several polls every week during the actual campaign – both at national and constituency level – but the months leading up to the dissolution of the Dáil also featured numerous polls.

Although politicians tend to play down their importance – describing them as 'a snapshot in time' or arguing that the 'real poll will be on election day' – there is no denying that polls are excellent indicators of how the election will turn out. For example, the constituency polls in the run-up to the 2007 election never tallied with the widespread predictions that Fianna Fáil would lose between ten and twenty seats.

The national polls, meanwhile, accurately showed a growth in support for Fianna Fáil during the election, while an *Irish Times* poll on the Monday before polling day – again disbelieved by some – was spot on in pointing to a consolidation in support for the two main parties, Fianna Fáil and Fine Gael. Even more accurate was the RTÉ exit poll, the results of which were released at 7am on the morning of the count.

The benefits of such polls have long been a source of debate.

Some commentators have criticised them for deflecting attention away from more important policy issues. The impact of the polls on the electorate's voting intentions has also been raised. For example, it seems likely that Fianna Fáil would have secured an overall majority in 2002 had a poll in a leading Sunday newspaper on the weekend before polling not shown the party heading for over 50 per cent of the first-preference vote.

The poll was clear evidence that what had come to be regarded as 'the impossible' – one party securing 83-plus seats – was not just possible but very, very probable. It seems inarguable that the poll result prompted some voters either not to vote or to switch their preference (the PDs with their 'One-Party Government? NO thanks' campaign was the biggest beneficiary).

It's not just voters who are influenced by opinion polls. In 2001, Fine Gael dumped its leader John Bruton, with disastrous consequences for the party, on the basis of poor opinion-poll ratings. Efforts were made by the Fianna Fáil–PDs government to restrict opinion polls during an election campaign. However, despite some strong arguments in favour, the move was quietly dropped after serious opposition emerged.

Opinion polls didn't always play such a key role in general elections. The first opinion poll in Ireland took place in the early 1960s. Labour undertook a major polling exercise in 1969 and there were a number of polls on party support in the 1970s, but they were generally rejected as 'unreliable'. If there was a turning point in the use of opinion polls, it came during the 1977 general election.

The Fine Gael and Labour coalition came into that election as virtually everybody's favourite to secure another term in office. A seemingly inevitable second election defeat for Fianna Fáil would surely result in the resignation of Jack Lynch and prompt a bitter power struggle between Charles Haughey and George Colley that threatened to rip Fianna Fáil asunder. No surprise then that many commentators were predicting that Fianna Fáil would be transformed into the natural party of opposition for the latter part of the twentieth century. Virtually every commentator predicted that the coalition would be returned and comfortably so.

There were some genuine reasons for optimism for the government. The economy was starting to recover after the disastrous consequences of the oil crisis. A budget, described by historian J.J. Lee as 'mildly indulgent', had been well received. Two by-elections in 1976 – in Donegal North-East and Dublin South-West – had shown strong support for the government. And the infamous Tullymander, by Local Government Minister Jim Tully (see Chapter 32), seemed to make it impossible for Fianna Fáil to win an overall majority.

Few grasped at this point that the government's disastrous handling of the resignation of President Cearbhall Ó Dálaigh the previous autumn would be so damaging come election time or that the Tullymander would seriously backfire or, most importantly, that the voters had simply become fed up with the government.

However, there was some evidence, for those who wanted to look, that all was not well for the coalition. In October 1976, a TV programme called *Survey* reported on an opinion poll that showed a substantial groundswell of support for Fianna Fáil. And two months later, the *Politics Programme* on TV reported on a series of 11 surveys, conducted by high-profile polling company IMS since late 1974, that showed a consistently widening margin in favour of Fianna Fáil (the sole exception being a survey conducted after the release of Dr Tiede Herrema, the Dutch industrialist who had been kidnapped). While the news of those surveys did make the front pages of the following day's newspapers, there was a general tone of scepticism about the findings. Opinion polls were still widely distrusted at this point.

THE DRAMA

There was a split in the cabinet over the timing of the election, with urban-based ministers, including Foreign Affairs Minister Garret FitzGerald, favouring holding on until near the end of the government's term of office in early 1978. They wanted to give the public some time to recognise the economic recovery that they believed was under way. However, Taoiseach Liam Cosgrave sided with those in favour of a June election. Nowadays, no government would dream of taking such a decision without recourse to private and public opinion polls, but not in 1977. In his autobiography *All in a Life*, Garret FitzGerald recalled that 'Liam Cosgrave was known to be particularly dismissive of polls, preferring rather oddly to be guided on public opinion by individual letters he received from time to time, extracts of which he sometimes read to us in government'.

FitzGerald said that the idea of commissioning a poll before deciding on a June election had struck him and a couple of other ministers. 'But we were inhibited from suggesting it by the dismissive reaction we believed we would have met from most of our colleagues, including the Taoiseach. Our inhibitions were akin to those we might have felt about proposing that we consult an astrologer.' (Interestingly, though, the coalition had pre-tested their policy package on a sample of the electorate prior to the 1973 general election.)

The election was duly called and the various ministers departed for their constituencies. An ad-hoc coalition election committee – made up of some Dublin-based ministers and a few aides – decided at this point to commission MRBI, another of the country's top polling companies, to carry out a nationwide poll with a sample of 600. The results were disastrous for the government, but it was clearly too late to postpone the election. The poll showed that 59 per cent of those who expressed a view said they intended to vote Fianna Fáil – which would give the opposition a landslide of unprecedented proportions. The margin in these private polls did narrow over the election campaign, but only by a few points.

However, all this time the public perception of a probable coalition victory remained because there was simply no empirical evidence to the contrary publicly available. The only report that did appear on opinion polls was a leaked, garbled and incomplete version of one set of results which, the reports said, suggested that the two sides had started the campaign with evenly balanced support and that the coalition had since gained a lead. One newspaper did commission a series of polls during the campaign but did not ask the direct question of how people intended to vote. Instead, the parties were assessed on a variety of factors. Fianna Fáil was crucially well ahead on the economy with the coalition having a narrow lead on Northern Ireland, security and social issues.

However, when asked which politician would make the best Taoiseach assuming a Fianna Fáil or coalition victory, 73 per cent said Lynch while only 44 per cent chose Cosgrave. A telling result that was not fully appreciated until after the votes were counted.

EPILOGUE

The election result showed the opinion polls carried out by IMS and MRBI were extremely accurate. Fianna Fáil – helped by a slick campaign and a manifesto packed with an enticing list of promises – secured an enormous 50.6 per cent of the first-preference vote and won a massive 20-seat majority in the Dáil. Instead of Jack Lynch resigning, it was the leaders of the two coalition parties – Liam Cosgrave and Brendan Corish – who quickly submitted their resignations. Three of their cabinet ministers also lost their seats. Contrary to the predictions, Fianna Fáil would continue to be the natural party of government – holding power for all bar seven of the following thirty years. Despite the evidence under their noses, nobody had seen it coming. From 1977 on, no leader or commentator would ever again ignore the importance, or doubt the relevance, of opinion polls.

12

Up the Poll
2002

PROLOGUE

The general election campaign of 2002 boiled down to just one question: Which party, if any, would join Fianna Fáil in government? With Fine Gael's credibility in tatters (see Chapter 26), Bertie Ahern was a racing certainty to be returned as Taoiseach. For months before the election, it was presumed that a Fianna Fáil/Labour coalition was the most likely option. However, as the election approached there were growing signs that an overall majority for Fianna Fáil, previously dismissed as an impossibility, was becoming very possible.

In contrast, the PDs – who had been in coalition government with Fianna Fáil for the previous five years of unprecedented economic prosperity – seemed to be in some difficulty heading into the election campaign. Only two of its four TDs were contesting the election and a series of constituency polls showed the party faring badly in traditional heartlands such as Limerick East, Galway West and Dublin South-East. Predictions that the party might win as few as three seats were commonplace.

As the campaign developed, the polls got better and better for Fianna Fáil, while the PDs were barely registering with just 2 per cent or 3 per cent. Fianna Fáil strategists, although aware that the party was on course for an overall majority, were anxious to play down this possibility, conscious that it might unnerve those voters who remembered the disastrous experience of the last time Fianna Fáil won an overall majority in 1977. That Fianna Fáil government allowed spending to run seriously out of control, and was the catalyst for a decade of high unemployment and emigration in the 1980s.

In order to reassure voters, Bertie Ahern went so far as to state publicly that he was in favour of going into government with the PDs, even if Fianna Fáil won an overall majority. Nobody could see such a scenario coming to pass – there was no doubt that if Fianna Fáil won 84-plus seats, it and it alone would be in government.

THE DRAMA

In press conferences, the PDs' leader Mary Harney continually warned that on the basis of the polls, Fianna Fáil was on course to win more than 90 seats. But many in the media remained sceptical about Fianna Fáil's chances of an overall majority. Something radical was needed to ram home the point to voters about the dangers of a Fianna Fáil landslide.

In his definitive book on the PDs – *Breaking the Mould: How the PDs Changed Irish Politics* – Stephen Collins wrote that the party's backroom team decided to confront the voters directly with this message in key target constituencies. Michael McDowell had returned to the party fold earlier in 2002 and was standing in Dublin South-East – the constituency where by then he had twice won and twice lost a seat. It was he who suggested abandoning a

12 – Up the Poll

planned media advertising campaign in favour of more old-fashioned lamp post posters, highlighting the importance of Fianna Fáil not getting an overall majority. All through the campaign McDowell had warned about the dangers of what PD strategists referred to as SPG (Single-Party Government).

He had strongly denounced Ahern's plan for a National Stadium at Abbotstown, comparing it to something from Ceauşescu's Romania. However, when the campaign entered its final week, McDowell really struck pay-dirt and secured his place in Irish electoral history. The future Tánaiste shinned up a lamp post near his home in Ranelagh to hang a poster declaring: 'One-Party Government? NO Thanks!' It was a stunt, and not a particularly dignified one at that, but it worked brilliantly, grabbing the attention of the print and broadcast media. As Collins wrote in *Breaking the Mould*, it also set the agenda for the final week of the campaign with the debate centred on whether Fianna Fáil ought to be in government on its own.

Just in case anyone was in any doubt as to the potential danger of single-party government Fianna-Fáil style, McDowell distributed a leaflet listing the reasons why it was undesirable. A one-party government could more easily cover up scandals and policy errors, McDowell warned. Nobody needed reminding of what had happened in the early and late 1980s when Fianna Fáil, under Charlie Haughey, had been in power on its own.

The campaign worked a treat. 'McDowell's plea to the electorate not to give Fianna Fáil an overall majority struck a chord with a significant number of voters and catapulted the PDs into a pivotal position during the final stages of the campaign. What McDowell's *démarche* showed was that even in the era of meticulously planned campaigns based on focus groups and continuous polling, it was still possible for a politician with flair and courage to take a campaign by the scruff of the neck and have a decisive impact on the final result,' wrote Collins.

EPILOGUE

There were fears within the PDs on the eve of the count that the strategy might have backfired, but they need not have worried. By the time the votes had been counted, the party had exceeded the most optimistic predictions, taking eight seats nationwide – double its 1997 total. Crucially, it had won two unexpected seats, in Galway West and Longford-Roscommon, that directly denied Fianna Fáil an overall majority.

Fianna Fáil missed out on that majority by less than 400 votes. The PDs were back in government with two full cabinet posts. They had achieved their goal of denying Fianna Fáil the opportunity to rule alone. The beauty of the campaign, led by McDowell, was that the PDs, despite being in government for the previous five years with Fianna Fáil, managed to portray themselves as the only real opposition to Fianna Fáil, the only real alternative to a Fianna Fáil overall majority.

The small party, whose very future was being questioned a few short weeks earlier, made itself relevant and put itself centre stage. And it did so by climbing up a lamp post.

13

The Agony and the Ex-TD – 1
1965

PROLOGUE

The system of single transferable votes (STV-PR) used in Irish elections, allied to the country's relatively small population, means that the outcome of a seat can regularly depend on a handful of votes, sometimes coming down to the ninth or tenth preference of a couple of voters. The tightness of the vote means that the formation of a government is invariably determined by a few hundred votes going in one direction rather than another. However, for those involved in the count, formation of a government is generally the last thing on their minds – understandably, their focus is on winning their seat.

The ten-day long Ben Briscoe–Eric Byrne marathon count in Dublin South-Central is remembered as the longest in the history of the State (see Chapter 14), but the general election of 1965 must still rank as having the most dramatic count.

The Ben and Eric Show was only one of a number of factors in the formation of a government in 1992. Even after the result in Dublin South-Central was announced, there were at least three different governments that could have been formed. However, in 1965 there were two marathon counts and a third very tight call, which had a serious bearing on the outcome of the general election.

Back then, Taoiseach Seán Lemass carried through on his threat to call a general election if his minority government lost a by-election in Cork. Fianna Fáil fought the general election based on its record in office and under the slogan 'Let Lemass Lead On'. Lemass's confidence that Fianna Fáil could win that April general election was borne out by a strong increase in his party's vote from 43.8 per cent to 47.8 per cent – the first time Fianna Fáil had ever increased its vote after a normal period in office (the party had previously done so only after calling snap elections).

However, despite a hefty increase in its first-preference vote, it quickly became clear that Lemass's ability to govern in the eighteenth Dáil would depend largely on the outcome of three long drawn-out counts: Dublin North-East, Longford-Westmeath and North Mayo. With those three counts still to come, the result stood at Fianna Fáil 71 seats, others 70 (with Fine Gael and Labour accounting for 67 of those).

Two seats out of three would give Lemass an overall majority, one would give him half the Dáil total – tight but enough to govern once the opposition was given the job of Ceann Comhairle. The loss of all three could potentially put Fine Gael and Labour, who ultimately gained six seats in the election, in with a chance of forming a government (although Labour had ruled out coalescing with any party).

THE DRAMA

It says something about the tightness and protracted nature of the two other counts that the result in North Mayo, where Fianna Fáil lost out on a seat by just 14 votes, was largely overshadowed by what happened in the other two constituencies. In Longford-Westmeath, former minister and War of Independence hero General Seán MacEoin was facing a major challenge from Paddy Lenihan, father of the then Minister for Justice Brian Lenihan. MacEoin took ill during the campaign and spent the remainder of the election in hospital. When the result of the count was announced, Lenihan was deemed elected, holding an advantage of just seven votes over MacEoin.

Meanwhile, over in Dublin North-East, there were just 11 votes between Labour's Denis Larkin and outgoing Fianna Fáil deputy Eugene Timmons. To complicate matters there, Fine Gael TD Patrick Byrne was also just marginally ahead of the two men.

At the count at the Temperance Hall in Longford, Fine Gael had drafted in its legal big-wigs – two senior counsels and two junior counsels – to supervise proceedings. They sought a full re-count of all the votes cast and when this was rejected by the returning officer, they said they would go to the High Court.

The Fine Gael barristers argued that an examination of the votes of Lenihan and running mate (and poll-topper) Frank Carter, carried out on the re-count, was not in accordance with the Electoral Acts of 1923 and 1963 because no proper examinations had been completed by the official enumerators to see if the ballot papers, passed for the two men, contained the official seal as required. They also claimed the ballot papers were not turned over by the enumerators so both sides could be seen by MacEoin's agents. The papers of Carter and Lenihan were dealt with so quickly that the tallymen didn't have time to examine the papers, the barristers argued.

Back in five-seat Dublin North-East, life was proving just as difficult. By the Sunday after the election – after four days of counting – only two candidates had been elected: Charlie

13 – The Agony and the Ex-TD – 1

Haughey and Fine Gael's Patrick Belton. A further three seats had to be filled. George Colley was a shoo-in for one of those, but for the remaining seats it was any two from three: Byrne, Timmons and Larkin. Fine Gael demanded a second check of Haughey's papers on the grounds that they were not sufficiently scrutinised for the official stamp. The returning officer agreed. The Fianna Fáil officials announced they would use magnifying glasses to scrutinise the papers. A full re-count was then ordered by the returning officer – the first ever held in the State's history. Before this election, only a re-count of the preceding count could be requested. However, a change in the Electoral Act allowed for a re-count of all votes cast.

By Tuesday, the sixth day of counting and re-counting, three seats in the new Dáil remained unfilled. Lenihan remained a slight favourite over MacEoin in Longford-Westmeath, but Timmons was drawing closer to Larkin in Dublin North-East.

The Temperance Hall looked more like the High Court with the count regularly halted to hear legal experts expound their views at round-table conferences on the stage. This was long before the days of the smoking ban – the minister who would introduce it was still only a child at this point – and the *Irish Press* reported that 'as the hours progressed and the counts trickled in, the number of empty cigarette ends on the hall floor swelled and the windows had to be opened for fresh air'. It also noted that the law books spread around the counting tables seemed to outnumber the votes.

On that Tuesday, 62-year-old Paddy Lenihan was deemed elected, defeating MacEoin by just 13 votes – unlucky for the general who had been a TD for 43 years. MacEoin was still in St Bricin's Military Hospital at that point – a fact that cost him at least one vote. One of the ballot papers that was disallowed was barred because, although it was otherwise perfectly marked, it also contained the words: 'God bless Seán MacEoin; may you get well soon.'

Probably due to exhaustion on everybody's part, the announcement of Lenihan's victory was received quietly. 'I am here by the skin of my teeth,' declared Lenihan. In thanking the legal men, he joked that when the count began most of them knew very little about PR, but now they knew so much they wanted it abolished. Fine Gael wasn't happy, complaining that the parcels of votes were not examined as had happened in Dublin North-East, and maintaining it would take a High Court challenge. But that challenge, even had it been taken, would have no impact on the Dáil's election of a Taoiseach because the rules are clear; when the new Dáil meets, all the deputies that have been declared elected by the returning officer have the right to vote on the new Taoiseach.

Meanwhile, back in Bolton Street College in Dublin, after seven days of counting, Patrick Byrne and Denis Larkin were elected. Timmons was only 25 votes behind Byrne and an agonising four votes adrift of Larkin. Timmons said it would all have been worth it if it showed up the chaos of proportional representation. Larkin called for an improvement in the mechanics of PR to eliminate the marathon counts.

Fianna Fáil had been narrowly beaten in Dublin North-East and North Mayo, but Lenihan's victory in Longford-Westmeath was enough to secure the party 72 out of the 144 seats and a working majority of one when a Ceann Comhairle was elected from the opposition benches. Seán Lemass no doubt reflected that another 20 votes would have been enough to give him a more comfortable four-seat majority. However, he also knew that a loss of a mere 13 votes might have potentially removed him from office, despite the party's strong first-preference vote.

EPILOGUE

Not surprisingly the long delays in the two constituencies prompted strong criticisms of PR and calls for a more straightforward system to be introduced. In the days after the count, Lemass said there was no enthusiasm for a change in PR, but that the government would look again at the 1963 Electoral Act. In fact, Fianna Fáil did attempt to change the system just three years later – by which point Lemass had been replaced as Taoiseach by Jack Lynch – when a referendum designed to abolish STV-PR was far more soundly defeated than an earlier attempt in 1959.

That 1965 election also threw up another first – Paddy Lenihan's election marked the first time that a father was elected to the Dáil when his son was already a member. Brian Lenihan was the first to shake his father's hand on his election. Lenihan Jnr had been re-elected for the adjoining constituency of Roscommon. Ironically, Paddy lived on the Roscommon side of the Shannon – outside his constituency's boundaries – while Brian lived on the Leinster side of the Shannon in his Dad's constituency. Neither men could vote for themselves and presumably they voted for each other. Another of Paddy's family – his daughter Mary O'Rourke – was elected to the Dáil from the same constituency 17 years later and went on to become a high-profile minister. Two of his grandchildren, Brian Jnr and Conor, were also elected to the Dáil and went on to hold ministerial office.

14

The Agony and the Ex-TD – 2
1992

PROLOGUE

The November 1992 election was a disaster for Taoiseach Albert Reynolds and Fianna Fáil. The electorate firmly blamed Fianna Fáil for the collapse of the Fianna Fáil-PD coalition and handed the party its worst electoral performance in over half a century. Fine Gael, under John Bruton, had an even more dismal election, losing ten seats and dropping to just 45. The Fine Gael result came despite widespread predictions by commentators before polling day of a Fine Gael-led coalition taking power after the election.

But if Fianna Fáil and Fine Gael had a bad election – dropping a combined 9.8 per cent in first-preference votes – Labour, under Dick Spring, had its best ever performance. The 'Spring Tide' delivered an increase of 9.9 per cent in the party's first-preference vote and more than a doubling of Labour seats to 33. The other two parties in the equation were the PDs, which enjoyed a good election coming out of government by increasing its Dáil representation to 10 from 6, and Democratic Left, which struggled with just 2.8 per cent of the vote.

The day after the count, the only thing that was clear was that it would be impossible to form a government without the newly powerful Labour party. There were all sorts of complications to the process of putting together a government. A Fianna Fáil-Labour government had seemed unthinkable before the election. Labour didn't want to be part of a coalition with the PDs, while Fine Gael wasn't particularly keen on Democratic Left. It also quickly became apparent that a huge amount hinged on the outcome of the last remaining count in Dublin South-Central, where Fianna Fáil was hoping to win its sixty-eighth seat of the election with Ben Briscoe, and Democratic Left was hoping to take a fifth seat with Eric Byrne. With a fifth seat for Democratic Left, the combined Fine Gael, Labour and Democratic Left strength would be 83, the tightest possible Dáil majority.

However, without the additional Democratic Left seat in Dublin South-Central, the parties wouldn't have the numbers to put together a working majority. It turned out that just five votes out of nearly 1.7 million would have a significant bearing on who became Taoiseach.

THE DRAMA

The significance of the count in Dublin South-Central may have been obvious fairly quickly, but that was the only speedy thing about what happened there. What ensued was the longest count in the history of the State, lasting ten days (98 hours) and involving six attempts to fill the seat. The margin between the two outgoing TDs was incredibly narrow and at no stage during the process was there more than ten votes between them.

The advantage swung between the two men like a pendulum. At 2.30am on the Friday after the Wednesday election, Briscoe was about to be declared elected by just nine votes. However, Democratic Left was granted a re-check and, later that day, the presiding officer said he was not satisfied with the result and ordered a re-count. The re-count took place over the weekend and on early Monday and turned up a different result. At 4am on the Monday, five days after counting began, Byrne was deemed to be elected by ten votes. But things were only just getting interesting (or perhaps irritating). Briscoe's director of elections demanded a re-count. There had been fairly significant changes in the figures. The total poll had dropped by 39 votes, the total valid poll was down by 43, but there was an extra 82 spoiled votes. Given these changes, there was even talk of Fianna Fáil seeking recourse to the High Court to demand a full re-count A returning officer was empowered under the 1991 Electoral Act to re-count all the papers, but the candidate is only entitled to a re-examination and a re-count which does not disturb the arrangement of the parcels of ballot papers unless an error has been discovered. The parcels are crucial as it is votes from the top of each sub-parcel that are selected for transfers.

A check of the votes the following day left less than five votes between the two men, with Byrne still holding the edge, but the returning officer said that a 'significant error' had been discovered which would be likely to affect the outcome and a full re-count was announced for 3 December.

Both Briscoe and Byrne had teams of supporters to help their cause, with members of the Kevin Barry Cumann in UCD drafted in by Fianna Fáil. The students certainly added to the atmosphere – at one point they were ordered to take down their party posters, including a picture of Seán Lemass, on the grounds that this was 'not a party convention'. There were about 100 supporters of Democratic Left from as far away as Cork, many of whom were taking time off work to help with the scrutinisation of the ballot papers. The contrast between the respective resources of Fianna Fáil and Democratic Left was summed up by media reports that the Democratic Left team lived on trays of sandwiches, while the Kevin Barry Cumann members were apparently given vouchers for full meals in the RDS restaurant.

But relations between the two sides were dignified at all times. Given the tension, this was a credit to all concerned, particularly Briscoe and Byrne. While the long-drawn-out process must have been unbearable for the two candidates, it was also gruelling for the enumerating team who were quickly dubbed 'the RDS 24'.

Although there was still a re-count scheduled for two days later, it did seem that Byrne held the advantage. Briscoe spent 1 December clearing out his Dáil office, which must have been some job after 28 years of politics.

The full re-count started, as planned, on 3 December, but was adjourned that night – the re-count had thrown up further readjustments in the number of spoiled votes. Briscoe later recalled that every time another vote was discovered in a bundle, it was greeted by his team of UCD students 'like scoring a goal for Ireland'.

The following Friday – after nine days and six attempts to fill the seat – the result of the re-count showed a further dramatic swing: Briscoe was ahead by five votes. But before he was declared elected, a re-check was granted to Byrne. However, this final re-check the next day – which threw up more disagreement over 'spoiled' ballot papers – showed four votes between the two, with Briscoe still ahead, and this was not deemed to be sufficient to overturn the result announced on Friday night. Briscoe, with 6,526 votes to Byrne's 6,521, was declared elected to wild cheers from the Kevin Barry Cumann. The Ben and Eric show had reached the final curtain. It was the first time in the State's history that the outcome of the original result was overturned.

The counting and re-counting had produced three different sets of results.

Such was the complexity involved that, during the fifth attempt to fill the seat, the City Sheriff brought in two experienced count supervisors – a solicitor from Arthur Cox Solicitors, who had served in 12 general-election counts, and a senior official in Dublin Corporation. Ballot papers marked with three Xs for the three Fianna Fáil candidates in the constituency were the more frequent spoiled votes affecting the result – which may have been due to confusion caused by the holding of the abortion referendum, with three separate votes, on the same day as the election.

In his magnanimous victory speech, Briscoe praised Byrne as a man of dignity. Byrne, in turn, said that Chinese drip-water torture had to be less painful than the agony he and Briscoe had endured over the previous ten days and jokingly asked voters in Dublin South-Central to 'please be more decisive next time when casting your votes'.

A Democratic Left member leaving the count centre lamented that Fianna Fáil's UCD students were there for the 'fun and excitement' and, while there was nothing wrong with that, 'we're here because of Democratic Left – it was so important for us to win the seat.' A member of the Kevin Barry Cumann joked that 'getting our names into the *Guinness Book of Records*' was a factor in their presence.

EPILOGUE

Recalling the events of that vote, 15 years on, Briscoe said that his son had been very ill at the time and he prayed to God 'take my seat, but don't take my son' – both survived. During the count process, Byrne had strongly argued for electronic voting to be introduced because the current antiquated system of counting was unacceptable, but some years later he said that, on reflection, he felt the whole process was 'very healthy democratically'.

The outcome of the marathon count ruled out any chance of a Rainbow coalition incorporating Fine Gael, Labour and Democratic Left. To everybody's surprise, Labour controversially opted to go into government with Fianna Fáil.

There was better news for Byrne 18 months later when he was returned to the Dáil after he won a by-election in the constituency caused by the resignation of Fianna Fáil's John O'Connell. By December 1994, the Fianna Fáil-Labour government collapsed and with the changed Dáil aritmetic, the Rainbow coalition had the votes it needed to form a government. Unfortunately for Byrne, he lost the seat again in 1997 and failed to regain it in 2002 or 2007. In fact, in 2007, once again he was cruelly on the wrong side of another very close count – losing by just 69 vote to Aengus Ó Snodaigh of Sinn Féin after yet another re-check of ballot papers!

15

Jack on the Box
1973

PROLOGUE

RTÉ television first started covering general elections in 1965. Before that, coverage of elections was dominated by newspapers with only scant coverage of the results on radio. However, it would be two general elections later before television's primacy on election night would really be established. Fianna Fáil faced into the 1973 election, having been in power, uninterrupted, for the previous 16 years and for 35 of the previous 41 years. Not surprisingly, given this record, there was a feeling that the party had been in power for too long, with suggestions that it was becoming arrogant.

However, it seemed as if the governing party would be facing an opposition in poor shape. Only a couple of months earlier, Fine Gael had been split down the middle when its leader, Liam Cosgrave, going against the majority view in his party, wanted to support tough anti-terrorist legislation introduced by Taoiseach Jack Lynch. Fine Gael seemed to be about to dump Cosgrave but just as the vote was about to take place on 1 December 1972, bombs, widely suspected to be the work of loyalists, exploded in the centre of Dublin – within earshot of the Dáil – and the Fine Gael TDs decided to support their leader and the legislation. The belief was that if the bombs hadn't exploded and Fine Gael had been split on the vote, Fianna Fáil would have gone virtually straight away to the country and, with Fine Gael in disarray, the outcome would have been inevitable. Labour, meanwhile, had voted against the anti-terrorist bill. The two opposition parties had also been on opposite sides during the 1972 referendum on joining the EEC, with Labour opposing Ireland's entry.

However, the desire to avoid another four or five years on the opposition benches meant that the two opposition parties surprised Fianna Fáil by getting their collective act together. Once the election was called, they agreed to offer the electorate an alternative government and brought out a joint 14-point plan (see Chapter 54). Fianna Fáil, in turn, tried to up its game by making promises on rates and social welfare, but the momentum was unmistakably with the opposition.

THE DRAMA

When RTÉ began its 1973 election-night broadcast, there was no inkling that history was about to made. Fianna Fáil's share of the first-preference vote actually increased in the election, and the combined Fine Gael/Labour vote dropped, but the coalition deal between the two parties resulted in an increase in transfers between the two opposition parties.

It was clear that Fianna Fáil had lost seats and the opposition had made gains when Taoiseach Jack Lynch took his seat in the studio. Presenter Brian Farrell, who became synonymous with RTÉ's election coverage, asked him if he was making any concessions or if he was waiting for the bitter end. Lynch opened up like he was going for the pat answer – the equivalent of a football manager saying he didn't see the incident when his star player dug his studs into an opposition player. 'In the first place,' he said, 'I haven't had the opportunity to review the scene. I've been going from one studio to another, between UTV, ITN and various Radio Éireann programmes, so I'm not *au fait* with the ultimate situation.'

So far, so expected. But then Lynch did something that no Irish leader of a government had ever previously done live on television: he conceded the election. His actual words were, 'but accepting the fact that we're not likely to exceed 70 seats, obviously the coalition will now form a government.' The election was over and it had been conceded on television.

EPILOGUE

It was a stunning moment of television, not least because with the election so tight – the coalition ended up with only a two-seat majority – Lynch could easily have kicked for touch when asked the question at that point. Consider how Fine Gael continued to insist that Enda Kenny could still be Taoiseach, despite all the evidence to the contrary, in the wake of the 2007 general election.

Brendan Halligan, Labour's general secretary at the time, was sitting to Lynch's right in the studio when he made his concession. Years later he told the RTÉ documentary on Brian Farrell's role in election coverage, *Lights, Camera, Farrell,* that in 'many ways it was the best moment of my life.'

'I just said to myself, isn't this a fantastic privilege – to live in a democracy? Here I am, power is passing from this man sitting on my left-hand side. There are no guns in the streets. There are no tanks. The people have spoken. It's a wonderful privilege to live

15 – Jack on the Box

through democracy.' It helps of course when you're on the winning side!

In the same programme, Farrell recalled how Lynch was very relaxed. 'He came in, had the pipe out, sat down and chatted. I pushed him. He didn't demur. He didn't make an issue out of it.'

He recalled that when Lynch finally did leave the studio that night, typical of his natural courtesy, he went around and shook hands with everybody. 'There was a sense of guilt from those who hadn't voted for him and almost a sense that if they had the chance again, maybe they would have voted Fianna Fáil.' Four years later, the nation would, in their droves.

16

Death on the Canvass – 1
1932

PROLOGUE

The general election of February 1932 was one of the most momentous in the State's history (see Chapter 38), marking the eclipsing of Cumann na nGaedheal by Fianna Fáil. Ever since this election, Fianna Fáil has had the highest first-preference vote in every general election.

The 1932 election was a bitter and, at times, violent election, with tensions increased by the IRA's decision to support Fianna Fáil. However, the most violent incident that occurred in this election, or in any since, had nothing to do with Civil-War politics. It resulted in the shooting dead of two men – one an outgoing TD/general-election candidate and the other a detective.

THE DRAMA

Just a couple of days before polling, Cumann na nGaedheal TD for Sligo–Leitrim, local merchant and farmer Patrick Reynolds, and Detective Officer Patrick McGeehan, were shot dead at Foxfield, near Ballinamore in Leitrim, by ex-RIC man Joseph

Leddy after an altercation in the latter's home. Leddy was charged with the murder of the two men. Back then justice was dispensed a lot quicker than today and within a couple of days a special court in Ballinamore began hearing evidence from eyewitnesses and the case was then quickly heard in the Central Criminal Court.

With the streets outside the court thronged with people, Francis MacNamee, a nephew of Leddy, told the Central Criminal Court his account of events. He was having dinner with Joseph Leddy and his family when Patrick Reynolds called to the door. Reynolds had been driving back from an election rally with three companions when he decided to call in to Leddy's. Although MacNamee said Reynolds was welcomed by both the accused and his wife, the TD immediately confronted Leddy with the words: 'You ____, you're out canvassing against me.' Leddy responded: 'I never went out canvassing agin you; I was always figuring on giving you number one.' According to MacNamee, Reynolds repeated the charge and then aimed a blow at Leddy. Leddy warned him not to 'come into my house to beat me or I will shoot you', to which Reynolds rather unwisely responded, 'I dare you to shoot me.' He then caught Leddy by the neck of his shirt and said, 'I'll kill you, you ____.'

The two men came to blows, at which point Detective Officer McGeehan and Michael Wrynne, two of Reynolds' four companions waiting in the car, heard the commotion and entered the house but the men left when Mrs Leddy ordered them out. Reynolds went out to the road before turning and saying to Leddy: 'You ____, I took a wrong oath to get you the pension, and by ____ I'll see you broke off it.' Leddy, who was standing in his doorway at this stage, warned the men not to return and went to get his gun. According to MacNamee, Reynolds and McGeehan approached the house again, with McGeehan warning Leddy:

'There are more guns than yours.' (A subsequent prosecution witness said that McGeehan added: 'I'll fire, Leddy, if you fire.') The judge later said that the evidence was conclusive that both men were facing Leddy. Leddy then shot McGeehan dead with his own gun, picked up the detective's revolver, unloaded it and handed it to MacNamee.

A few days after MacNamee's evidence, the court heard from those who had been in the car with Reynolds and McGeehan. Wrynne said he and his companions, including McGeehan, were waiting outside Leddy's house after Reynolds entered it. They heard raised voices as Reynolds and Leddy 'came to grips' with each other.

Wrynne claimed that it was at this stage that he and McGeehan entered Leddy's house and went into the kitchen. He also maintained that there had been no threat from Reynolds to Leddy, but he had heard Leddy threaten Reynolds.

A third companion of Reynolds, lawyer Barry O'Mahony who had earlier addressed a Cumann na nGaedheal rally with Reynolds in Carrick-on-Shannon, said that after McGeehan had been shot, Reynolds ran towards the back of their car, before turning towards Leddy's house and shouting: 'You need not think you will frighten me with your gun. I was never frightened. I faced better men than ever you were.'

At this point, Leddy fired his second shot, which fatally wounded Reynolds. O'Mahony said the accused looked down at the breach of his gun and gave 'a wild sort of laugh'. O'Mahony then ran to Leddy, shouting 'don't shoot, we are unarmed' to which Leddy replied: 'Are you CID too? Produce your gun.' O'Mahony insisted he was not CID and that he had no gun. He begged Leddy not to reload his gun. 'With every shot you have fired, you have brought down a man.' According to O'Mahony,

Leddy responded: 'I have, and I will shoot you too. Who are you and what brought you here?' O'Mahony explained why he was there and pleaded with Leddy, saying that he had never done him any harm.

The two men argued for about ten minutes. Although he was urged to leave the house by a woman present at the scene (who also told Leddy: 'You have shot enough men for today'), O'Mahony said he couldn't leave 'that madman with a gun when the guards were coming'. However, he got a barrel of the gun in the chin and a whack under the heart with its butt, as well as a 'box or two in the face', for his troubles.

O'Mahony testified that Leddy started to reload the gun, but was stopped by one of the women and O'Mahony ran to a nearby house. Leddy went back into the house, bolting the door. He then sent one of his children for a priest; Reynolds, who lay dying on the ground outside Leddy's house, had called for a priest and for Leddy to lift him, but according to O'Mahony, the accused stayed in the kitchen, walking up and down with the gun in his hands.

A local priest also gave evidence, saying that when he arrived to give the last rites Leddy said to him, 'This is a terrible thing but it had to be done. They came into my house to beat me.' The priest attempted to calm him down by suggesting it was an accident. Leddy agreed: 'There was a struggle and the gun went off.' The priest noted that when the guards arrived, Leddy had his two hands in his pockets and was smoking a pipe.

Leddy, who pleaded not guilty to murder, also gave evidence. He told how he had been a victim of an assault over a decade earlier when arresting a man in his capacity as an RIC man and how he had been struck on the forehead with a brick and on the back of the head with his own baton. He had spent six weeks in hospital and since then he had been short-tempered. He had received a pension from the Free State for services rendered to the IRA after he had retired from the RIC (he had gifted them a revolver and instructed men in drill). He said it was principally General Sean MacEoin, a Cumann na nGaedheal minister and War of Independence hero (see Chapter 13), who got him his pension, but Reynolds had always claimed credit, and 'I never contradicted it.' While he had canvassed for an independent candidate before, in 1927 he was a Reynolds supporter.

He claimed in court that on the day in question Reynolds had called him a liar and 'made a box' at him, threatening: 'By ____ I will kill you in your own house,' to which Leddy responded: 'If you come to kill me, Paddy, I will shoot you.' Leddy also claimed McGeehan had drawn out his revolver with the warning: 'Keep quiet you, Leddy,' and that Reynolds had reached for McGeehan's gun saying: 'By ____ I will plug him in his own door.'

Leddy said that at the time he fired, his nephew and his wife were pulling him down and that he had no intention of killing the two men; he thought he was going to be shot himself and was only acting in defence of his life and his family. He further claimed he had received a serious beating from detectives after his arrest. The defence team tried to paint Reynolds as a 'blackguard' with characteristics attained on the docks in New York (he had been a successful amateur boxer in the US which hardly made him a 'blackguard'), who had 'polluted the ears' of Leddy's wife with his bad language. It claimed Detective Officer McGeehan had entered the house as an aggressor.

On 10 March, less than a month after the tragic incident, the jury in Dublin's Central Criminal Court, after considering the facts of the case for less than two hours, found Leddy not guilty of murder, but guilty of manslaughter and, according to the media reports 'recommended him to mercy on account of the great provocation he received'. The presiding judge, Justice Meredith, said he agreed entirely with the verdict and the rider. He sentenced Leddy to '12 months simple imprisonment' in each case, with the two sentences to run concurrently. The jury also asked the judge to write to the Minister for Justice conveying its recommendations to mercy, in the hope that Leddy would not lose his pension.

EPILOGUE

Thousands of people attended the funeral on 17 February 1932 of 45-year-old Reynolds, who was a father of seven children, and all businesses in the Ballinamore area closed. Hundreds more visited the church where his body had lain since the day after he was shot. The coffin, wrapped in a tricolour, was borne to the hearse by Reynolds' comrades in the Ballinamore branch of the Knights of Columbanus.

Although it was a shocking incident, it appeared to have little impact on the election nationally (some posters reportedly appeared in South Mayo insinuating Fianna Fáil were in some way to blame for Reynolds' death, but the charge was too outlandish to be taken seriously). In the aftermath of the shooting, de Valera expressed his sympathy, but noted that in the press reports there was 'a certain inclination' to make political capital out of the tragedy. Everyone knew the issues of the election and they had nothing to do with this tragedy, de Valera said. Of course, the dreadful shooting dead of the TD and his companion did have one obvious impact on the general election.

Under the 1923 Electoral Act, the notice for a poll in the constituency had to be countermanded after the death of Reynolds and proceedings commenced afresh. Polling was set instead for early March, two weeks after the rest of the country voted. Reynolds' grieving widow, Mary, was nominated to stand in his place and won a seat, garnering 5,317 votes, nearly 1,400 more than her late husband had received five years earlier. She lost the seat in the 1933 general election but regained it four years later and held it until 1961. Rarely, if ever, can a candidate have won a seat in more traumatic circumstances. However, while Mary Reynolds polled strongly, the result in the Sligo–Leitrim constituency reflected the national swing, with Fianna Fáil taking four of the seven seats (compared to the two it had held before the election). This brought its seat total to 72, short of an overall majority but with a clear 15-seat lead over Cumann na nGaedheal.

A week after the Sligo–Leitrim poll, de Valera was elected President of the Executive Council with the help of Labour. Cumann na nGaedheal had lost office after ten years but, much more seriously, one of its candidates had lost his life in the momentous general election of 1932.

17

Cleaning Up After the Election
1932

PROLOGUE

The general election of 16 February 1932 was a defining one in Irish political history. After a decade of government by the pro-Treaty Cumann na nGaedheal, the general election was won by Fianna Fáil – a party formed by many of those who had been defeated in the Civil War. And once the party tasted power, it made it its business to hold on to it. Over the next 75 years, Fianna Fáil would be out of office for less than 18 years, making them arguably the most successful political party in Western democracy. The election of 1932 was even more crucial for another reason. It effectively copperfastened, for ever, the new state's democratic ethos. Despite fears of a military coup in opposition to Fianna Fáil taking office, William T Cosgrave and Cumann na nGaedheal, to their enormous credit, ensured a smooth handover of power to their arch-enemies. However, despite this wonderful exercise in democracy at a time when the dark clouds of totalitarianism were beginning to gather across continental Europe, not everybody in Ireland was happy.

17 – Cleaning Up After the Election

THE DRAMA

Less than two weeks after polling day, a furious column under the byline J.A.P. (bylines were extremely rare in those days) appeared in the *Irish Independent*. The journalist in question wasn't inflamed by the nation's ingratitude towards Cumann na nGaedheal or the shooting dead of a TD just days before the election (see Chapter 16). No, his beef (we're presuming it was a 'he') was how the election had 'disfigured the landscape'.

Under the headline: 'Cleaning up after the Election: The Disfigurations Scandal', he opened: 'The general election has left its mark on the country and I think steps should be taken immediately to remove it.' Politicians, he went on, accuse each other of trying to blacken the country, 'but what about the people who daubed it white, not to mention red and yellow?'

White of course was the popular colour of the political slogan painter because, as J.A.P. noted, 'it is so easy to make whitewash that it is generally used in rural districts to blacken the character of the opposite party.' He accepted that in the cities an appeal by the main parties to their followers to 'restrain their ardour for painting war cries on walls and gable ends' had some measure of success, but alas not in the countryside. 'Only at election times, the small boy spirit which lurks in every normal man gets a chance to indulge once more in the fine old sport of defacing someone else's property. When the man is amenable to discipline, he may contrive to suppress the small boy. Otherwise the *"enfant terrible"* bursts forth with a whoop of joy and proceeds to disfigure the landscape,' the writer thundered.

But he was only drawing breath at this point. 'Throughout the country, you will find the marks that the election has left – "Up

Doodlebunk!", "Vote for Macrahanish!" and similar inspiring signs staggering over walls and gates in huge white letters like the work of a gargantuan ghost afflicted with a bad attack of writer's cramp.' To be fair, he could write could J.A.P.

And it wasn't just those armed with a paintbrush that drew his ire – oh no! 'Flyposting' was 'another affliction', he fumed, raging against the bill sticker who goes around 'seeking places ornamented with the notice "post no bills" and then joyously covers all the available spaces with posters.' It was called 'flyposting', he explained, because a man 'has to be very "fly" to avoid being caught.'

In this regard, small bill stickers were 'peculiarly pestiferous' in the 1932 election, sticking candidates' 'hand-bill harangues on streetlamps, tramway standards, garage doors, garden gates, everywhere, regardless of the laws of property or common decency.'

It particularly irked the writer that the executioners of this 'deadly work' would get off without even a caution and he gave a quick insight into what life would be like in the Republic of J.A.P. – if it were ever formed. 'It is a good thing for these people that I am not head of the government in this country. Personally, I think that "something slow with boiling oil in it" would be a mild punishment for them,' he wrote, presumably (hopefully!) with his tongue firmly lodged in his cheek.

On a slightly more moderate note, he added that at the very least, an act should be passed as soon as the new Dáil meets to put an end to their activities by forcing wrongdoers to repair their damage. 'I would like to see the opposition, in the face of outraged public opinion, that would dare to oppose such a measure.' The writer argued that candidates and election agents should be held responsible for any disfigurement of public or private property 'by

17 – Cleaning Up After the Election

their too-zealous supporters'.

EPILOGUE

J.A.P.'s methods – particularly the boiling oil – might have sounded somewhat extreme, but he would no doubt be delighted with the strict rules that exist today whereby political parties are fined if they don't take down their election posters within a number of days of the election. No doubt he would have been in sympathy with those people who rang in to radio phone shows after the 2007 general election campaign to complain that political parties had pulled down the posters but failed to remove the plastic tags that had secured them. Seventy-five years on, Fianna Fáil in government and people bemoaning the election campaign's visual scarring of the nation: *plus ça change, plus c'est la même chose.*

18

Fine Gael's Lowest Ebb
1945

PROLOGUE

Fine Gael has always played second fiddle to the bigger, more dominant Fianna Fáil. While its predecessor, Cumann na nGaedheal, did hold power for the first ten years of the new state, it was swept aside by a brash and energetic new Fianna Fáil party and it has largely been playing catch-up ever since. There have been times, however, when Fine Gael seemed to be on the brink of taking over the mantle of the natural party of government.

When Fianna Fáil lost the 1973 election to Fine Gael and Labour's national coalition of 'all talents', many were forecasting that Fianna Fáil would need to get used to the opposition benches. But we all know what happened four years later in the 1977 general election (see Chapters 11 and 19). Fine Gael leader Garret FitzGerald came closest to bridging the gap between the two main parties.

His popularity and charisma were a major factor in this, but it was no coincidence that Fine Gael's best ever election performance came when it was facing Charlie Haughey, a hugely divisive figure in Irish politics. In the election of November 1982 (see Chapters 20 and 44), Fine Gael won 70 seats to come within just 5 seats of Fianna Fáil. However, as in 1973, the party had the bad luck to come into power during an economically dismal period. With the public finances in disarray and two coalition parties unable to agree on how to address the country's many problems, the government lost the confidence of the people.

It was no surprise that Fine Gael lost power (and 20 seats) in the general election of 1987. Incredibly the party has now gone a quarter of a century without winning a general election – its brief period in office between the end of 1994 and mid-1997 came after the Fianna Fáil-Labour government collapsed mid-term.

The party's meltdown in the 2002 general election (see Chapter 26) sparked predictions that Fine Gael's demise might be just another election away. However, Enda Kenny's leadership pulled the party back from the brink and, astonishingly, he came within three or four seats of toppling Bertie Ahern in the 2007 general election (although obviously he would have needed the support of Labour, the Greens and others to do so).

Those of us who believed the end might be nigh for Fine Gael after 2002 had ignored the lessons of history. Fine Gael may struggle to get into government – in the 74 years since its foundation it has been in power for less than 18 years – but it has always proved remarkably durable, seeing off pretenders for the number two slot in Irish politics and rattling Fianna Fáil from time to time. And Fine Gael activists can take consolation from the fact that if the party survived the 1943–1948 crisis, it can probably survive anything.

THE DRAMA

For the lowest point in Fine Gael's history, look no further than 4 December 1945. On that day, five by-elections – Clare, Dublin

North-West, Kerry South, Mayo South and Wexford – took place. Incredibly, Fine Gael, the main opposition party, contested just one of those five constituencies. As Michael Gallagher and Michael Marsh noted in their book on Fine Gael, *Days of Blue Loyalty*, the party 'was simply unable to find credible candidates to stand in four of them and had to stand aside'. The one it did contest, Clare, had been a Fine Gael seat, but the party was roundly thumped in the by-election, with Fianna Fáil winning about three times the vote of the Fine Gael candidate.

Not surprisingly, an orderly queue of political observers was forming to predict the party's speedy demise. While this date represented the party's undoubted nadir, the decline had been in train for some time. In the 1938 general election, Fianna Fáil won almost 52 per cent of the vote (see Chapter 38), its best ever election performance. Fine Gael, despite being the governing party as recently as six years earlier (when it was called Cumann na nGaedheal), put forward less candidates for that election (76, down from 95 in the election a year earlier) than the number of seats Fianna Fáil actually won (77). It was a declaration of intent, or rather lack of it. The fact that virtually all of its candidates would need to be elected for it to form a government on its own was clear evidence that the party did not think there was the remotest chance of this happening.

In the 1943 general election, although the other opposition parties made up some ground on Fianna Fáil, Fine Gael didn't make any headway. In fact, its vote dropped 10 percentage points and it lost 13 seats. It now had just 32 seats, less than half Fianna Fáil's total for the first time ever. A number of its big names – Richard Mulcahy and John A. Costello – lost their seats in that election. And it wasn't as if there was plenty of new talent coming in to fill their shoes. In the whole of the 1940s, future Taoiseach

Liam Cosgrave – son of William T Cosgrave – was practically the only newcomer to the Fine Gael benches.

Things got even bleaker in the snap general election of 1944. Fine Gael dropped another two seats to 30 and even lost William T Cosgrave's old seat in Cork. This time the party had nominated just 55 candidates. Although this was partly because a number of former Fine Gael TDs and candidates were running as independents, it demonstrated little confidence that Fianna Fáil could be unseated. During the actual campaign, it was noticeable that Fine Gael candidates minimised party affiliation. In the actual voting, internal transfers between Fine Gael candidates were low. The only consolation was the return to the Dáil of new party leader Richard Mulcahy who, after losing his seat twice in the previous three elections in Dublin North–East, changed constituency to Tipperary and was comfortably elected. There was more bad news for the party in November of 1944 when it failed to hold its seat in Kerry South in a by-election – the party now had just 29 TDs and, by the end of that Dáil, the figure would be only 28.

The future seemed bleak. De Valera and Fianna Fáil appeared invincible. Clann na Talmhan had won 13 and 11 seats respectively in the elections of 1943 and 1944. Fine Gael's organisation seemed moribund. It didn't engage in any fundraising and failed even to use the propaganda favoured by Cumann na nGaedheal (e.g. the 'Red Scare' tactics of 1932 – see Chapter 45). Its image – anti-nationalist and pro-Commonwealth – was poor.

In that bleak month of December 1945 – when the party could only contest one out of five by-elections – things were so bad that Mulcahy asked each TD and senator to bring ten members to the following year's Ard Fheis with them, as he believed that particular conference to be of vital importance. In *Days of Blue*

Loyalty, Gallagher and Marsh describe what happened at the meeting: 'In a discussion, that is scarcely credible for the main opposition party of the day, several TDs said they would do their best (before in some cases leaving the meeting for more pressing engagements) and by the end, only six Oireachtas members had promised to bring the required numbers.' Gallagher and Marsh also note that photos of Fine Gael Ard Fheiseanna from this period 'show small numbers of delegates, well wrapped up in coats, sitting glumly (often underneath constituency sign boards) in what appear to be cold and largely empty halls'.

It was probably Mulcahy, a largely forgotten politician of immense stature (see Chapter 10), more than anybody – aside perhaps from Lady Luck – who saved Fine Gael. He simply refused to accept the suggestion that Fine Gael served no purpose. He strived to present a more confident and assertive image for the party and brought through new policies. Despite this, Fine Gael went into the 1948 election largely written off. It did have 82 candidates – a more much credible number for the main opposition party – but only 22 of its TDs were running again, less than half the number elected ten years earlier. Little wonder those ten years have been described as the most dismal decade in Fine Gael's history.

The 1948 election was presented as a battle between a tired Fianna Fáil and the vibrant new force on the scene, Clann na Poblachta. Fine Gael was relegated to the status of a virtual also-ran. And sure enough, the party did not have a good election – it dropped below 20 per cent for the first and only time in its history. However, it benefited from a huge slice of luck with Fianna Fáil's redrawing of the constituencies. The government revision of the constituencies had been carried out with the rising Clann na Poblachta in mind. While it succeeded in limiting the Clann's gains, it had the undesirable (from Fianna Fáil's point of view) side effect of helping Fine Gael hold its head above water (see Chapter 32). Fine Gael's 31 seats were nothing to get excited about, but it was still by some margin the second biggest party and, because so little had been expected, it was seen as a positive result. It was described in one national newspaper as 'a remarkably firm stand by Fine Gael'.

And things were to get even better for the party. Fianna Fáil's seat numbers had dropped in the election but, despite its minority position, everyone still expected de Valera to put together a government. However, there was a desire among the rest of the Dáil to create an alternative to Fianna Fáil after it had been in power for 16 years. Mulcahy succeeded in doing the impossible: putting together the ultimate dolly-mixture coalition. It was made up of the pro-Commonwealth Fine Gael, the ultra-republican Clann na Poblachta, Labour and National Labour – who had been at each other's throats – along with Clann na Talmhan and a bevvy of independents (one of whom secured a seat at cabinet). Mulcahy then made the ultimate sacrifice for the party he had saved from virtual extinction. Because of his role in the Civil War, Clann na Poblachta would not accept him as Taoiseach, so he stepped aside to allow his Fine Gael colleague, John A. Costello, become Taoiseach.

EPILOGUE

There's an old saying that nothing succeeds like success and it certainly proved the case for Fine Gael. The 1948 inter-party government lasted only three years, but it transformed Fine Gael's fortunes. The party became relevant again, helped by a reinvigorated and properly financed organisation (it began a national collection in 1949).

While Fianna Fáil was back in government in 1951, Fine Gael gained nine seats in that election, as its vote rose by six percentage points. By the general election of 1954, Fine Gael had 50 seats (just 15 behind Fianna Fáil) and 32 per cent of the vote – 60 per cent up on its 1948 performance. It formed another coalition government after that election. While it lost seats in the election of 1957 and would remain out of government for the next 16 years, its support rose steadily during that time. There was no more talk about Fine Gael's imminent demise.

And crucially, the very notion of the party not contesting a by-election – as happened in four separate constituencies on 4 December 1945 – would never again be contemplated.

19

Inflation Once Again
1977

PROLOGUE

The 1973–1977 national coalition was dogged with bad luck during its time in office. The international economic climate was dreadful as a result of the oil crisis, which had a huge adverse impact on prices and consumer confidence. Rising prices and unemployment certainly damaged the government's popularity – its Minister for Finance, Richie Ryan, was famously dubbed 'Richie Ruin, the Minister for Hardship' by RTÉ's legendary political satire TV programme *Hall's Pictorial Weekly*.

However, by the time the general election came around in June 1977, ministers could point to some progress in the economy: inflation was falling, the economy was growing again and foreign borrowing had been reduced.

However, as those ministers who had argued for the election to be put off until later in the year understood, it would take time for the electorate, who had lived through some difficult years, to acknowledge those improvements. What the government certainly didn't need was an independent source questioning the progress it had been making – yet that is exactly what happened, just as the country was about to go to the polls.

19 – Inflation Once Again

THE DRAMA

Virtually on the eve of the election in 1977, research emerged from a little-known UK consultancy group saying that inflation in the twelve months to the end of May just gone had come to 18.1 per cent – four percentage points higher than the coalition was anticipating. The survey also claimed that the rate of Irish price inflation, excluding housing, was accelerating rather than slowing down. It said that for the four-month period to the end of May the increase in prices, excluding housing, was 9.5 per cent. And, on that basis, the inflation rate could be 20 per cent by September.

This research directly contradicted the coalition's message that inflation was slowly but surely being brought under control and that single-digit inflation could be expected from mid-1978. From the government's point of view, the timing could not have been worse. The survey was front-page news across the national newspapers right before election day. Fianna Fáil had already accused the government of delaying price rises until after the election and the survey gave it another stick with which to beat them.

Fianna Fáil leader Jack Lynch said that it had become clear in the past few days that 'official information on prices, unemployment and house-building has been concealed and manipulated'. His finance spokesman, George Colley, said the survey showed prices were 'not only out of control but getting worse' and the report 'must have a devastating effect on the wafer-thin credibility of the government'.

Justin Keating, Minister for Industry and Commerce, hit back saying the inflation forecast bore 'no relationship to reality' and the projection of 9.5 per cent inflation for the four months just gone was 'quite absurd'. Keating rejected the survey's finding that consumer prices in the Republic were 10 per cent higher than in the UK and 6 per cent higher than in the North, pointing to figures that showed a basket of goods, minus meat, was cheaper in Dublin than in London or Belfast. Another senior minister, Garret FitzGerald, said the survey was 'not a serious document', adding that its composition was heavily biased towards the richer sections of the community.

The managing director of the UK consultancy company that had produced the survey acknowledged that because the price of housing was not included in the index, he expected the official rate of inflation to be somewhat below his company's figure. But the story was a PR disaster for the government just as voters were about to go to the polls.

EPILOGUE

A look back at the inflation figures for 1977 shows that the coalition was right when it said that the inflation rate was coming down. The second-quarter figure – to the end of May – was 13.7 per cent, actually slightly below what the government had been predicting. Far from rising to 20 per cent by September, over the following two quarters the inflation rate fell to 13.5 per cent and then to 10.7 per cent. It hit single figures, 8.6 per cent, by the first quarter of 1978.

However, while the official figures vindicated what the coalition had been saying, in political terms it didn't matter because by that stage the election was long over and the pre-polling day argument had been forgotten by the vast majority of the electorate. By that point, Fine Gael and Labour were on the opposition benches, morosely observing the huge numbers of Fianna Fáil TDs sitting opposite them on the government side. The magnitude of the Fianna Fáil victory – not to mention the private polls that emerged later showing the coalition trailing miserably from the start of the campaign – means it would most definitely be an exaggeration to say the survey was a decisive factor in the general election result. The people were clearly fed up with the government and invigorated by the energy of the ultra-modern Fianna Fáil campaign, not to mention the range of extravagant promises the party was offering.

Nonetheless, the survey on prices certainly didn't help Fine Gael and Labour, undermining their already shaky economic record and possibly adding to a perception that there was no end in sight to rampaging inflation. Some commentators believe that it may particularly have been a factor in some of the three-seat Dublin constituencies, where Fianna Fáil surprisingly cleaned up.

Justin Keating was one of the ministers who lost his seat in the Fianna Fáil landslide and he blamed his defeat on being publicly associated with price rises during his tenure as minister. Perception is everything in politics, particularly at general election time.

20

Three Rounds of Charlie v Garret
1981 – 1987

PROLOGUE

Two men dominated Irish politics in the 1980s: Charles Haughey and Garret FitzGerald. It is arguable as to whether Irish politics has had, before or since, a bigger rivalry. There tended to be no middle ground when it came to views of Haughey during his time as leader of Fianna Fáil. The electorate was divided down the middle. Meanwhile, 'Garret the Good' brought Fine Gael to previously undreamed-of electoral highs – although it was surely no coincidence that this success came when the controversial Haughey was leader of Fianna Fáil.

Despite the often fanatical loyalty he attracted, Haughey was viewed by many in his own party as an electoral liability. Yet despite considerable evidence for that assertion, it is also true that no Fianna Fáil leader since has been able to match his record of attracting first-preference votes nationally. The rivalry between the two leaders kicked off in earnest on the night Haughey become party leader and Taoiseach in late 1979. In his speech as leader of the opposition, FitzGerald, infamously or accurately, depending on your viewpoint, referred to Haughey's 'flawed pedigree' and stated that people within Fianna Fáil and observers outside the party 'have attributed to him [Haughey] an overweening ambition which they do not see as a simple emanation of a desire to serve but rather as a wish to dominate, even to own the state'. Their rivalry lasted until February 1987 when FitzGerald stepped down as Fine Gael leader, having lost the general election. There were four general elections during the period (including three in a period of 18 months) and despite the woeful economic environment and the argument that the political system was failing its people, it was an era when politics gripped the nation.

Interest was never higher than in the three televised debates between the two main protagonists. Televised debates between the two main contenders had been a feature of other Western democracies for years. The encounter between John F. Kennedy and Richard Nixon in America as far back as 1960 was regarded as a defining point in that election, but the Irish public had to wait until 1982 for its first experience of a leaders' debate.

THE DRAMA

Act I

In the general election of June 1981, efforts to get Haughey and FitzGerald to square off came to nothing, although there was a highly unsatisfactory TV debate involving all the party leaders. But when FitzGerald's minority government was defeated in a budget vote the following January and another election ensued, the momentum for a televised head-to-head proved unstoppable. On Tuesday, 16 February, two days before polling day, the first TV debate between the two alternatives for Taoiseach took place with legendary broadcaster Brian Farrell as moderator.

The debate generated considerable excitement. That morning's *Irish Times*' front-page story was headlined 'TV debate could be crucial to poll result'. Both men were greeted on their arrival at Montrose by the cheers of enthusiastic supporters and the face-off was beamed by satellite to the US and Canada for news bulletins there the following day. FitzGerald went into the debate with a 23-point opinion-poll lead over Haughey in terms of personal popularity, although more importantly Fianna Fáil was five points ahead of Fine Gael and Labour. However, with a dire approval rating of just 33 per cent, Haughey needed a good performance in the debate to rehabilitate him, and he got it.

FitzGerald did score some points against Haughey, particularly when he asserted that in the Haughey government's 1981 budget a year earlier, expenditure had been notionally slashed by IR£100m without any policy decisions being taken to achieve that result. He also said the Central Bank had refused Haughey's government an overdraft of IR£350 million. In both cases, FitzGerald recalled in his autobiography *All in a Life*, he had documentary proof in front of him which the viewers could see. 'He was rattled by these accusations, which he nevertheless denied flatly,' FitzGerald said.

However, despite these telling points, FitzGerald generally appeared ill-at-ease and weary after his extensive tour of the country. FitzGerald himself recalled in *All in a Life* that 'knowing how much hangs on an occasion like this, and conscious of how one misplaced word can prove disastrous in such a gladiatorial contest, I was tense and probably showed it more than he did'.

The next day's *Irish Times* noted that 'the camera angles were kinder to Mr Haughey', and Haughey's more aggressive debating style gave him a decided edge. The *Times*' assessment was that what FitzGerald 'lacked in rhethoric' he made up for in detail, while Haughey's more pugnacious approach was not as specific. The Fianna Fáil leader was more confident and more emphatic on the defence of the Republic's ethos, it added. Haughey had attacked FitzGerald's constitutional crusade for increasing unionist intransigence by presenting them with 'a stick to beat us'.

An *Irish Independent* poll conducted hours after the debate was over was pretty emphatic, showing that 51 per cent of people believed Haughey had won the debate, compared to 35 per cent for FitzGerald. According to the poll, he was also ahead by 2:1 on confidence, being easier to understand and on debate prowess. However, there was some consolation for FitzGerald in that he was ahead by even bigger margins on credibility, honesty and reliability.

The general consensus was that Haughey's better performance was of greater benefit to him since his low ratings in the polls meant he could only move up. While the debate was deemed by the *Irish Times* editorial to be a 'fair success', one of its high-profile journalists, John Healy, said it all 'came perilously close to being the yawn of the election'. Along with the debate, Haughey won the election, although with just 81 seats out of 166, his minority government would find it difficult to survive.

Act II

Nine months later, the two men were back at it again when Haughey's very troubled government fell. There had been some doubt as to whether the debate would go ahead. Fine Gael – which had least to gain from the debate given that it and Labour were leading in the opinion polls – in particular quibbled over the terms. However, agreement was reached and there was exhaustive newspaper coverage of the event, which effectively ended the campaign. There was some controversy when FitzGerald refused to attend a photo call. The *Irish Press* reported that an 'irate' FitzGerald, 'obviously angered' by recent 'personal attacks' from

Haughey, had refused a handshake, which the paper's editorial said was 'a pity'.

In broadcaster John Bowman's assessment of the media coverage of the event, written for *Ireland at the Polls, 1981, '82 and '87 – A Study of Four General Elections*, he wrote: 'What was clear was that Fine Gael strategists, hoping that the bitterness of Haughey's attacks in recent days would swing votes in their direction, did not wish to confuse the party leaders' images by a widely publicised handshake.'

FitzGerald explained his reason for declining the handshake was for fear that it would all 'look like the beginning of a prize fight' and he did not want the debate 'to be seen as something to do with pugilism'. However, in his autobiography he added that one of his advisors suggested that turning down the proposed photo call might 'have the additional advantage of disconcerting my opponent just before our encounter. With this consideration also in mind, I delayed my entry to the studio until immediately before the broadcast was due to start'.

During the debate, Haughey notably failed to repeat some of his recent accusations against FitzGerald (see Chapter 44). Bowman wrote that 'Haughey's advisors explained that they did not want "a slanging match", hence his reluctance to repeat the charge that FitzGerald had been "a collaborator" with the British over policy toward Northern Ireland'.

FitzGerald scored a number of points over Haughey. On the economy, he refuted Haughey's claims that his national plan had been endorsed by the Central Bank, the ESRI and the European Commission and led him into disclaiming responsibility for the high spending of the Jack Lynch-led Fianna Fáil government of 1977 to 1979, despite being a member of the cabinet. On the North, Haughey accused FitzGerald of proposing a 'British-Irish

20 – Three Rounds of Charles v Garret

The Great Debate

force' to police Ireland. But he was unable to sustain the allegation when FitzGerald handed him a copy of his speech on the subject and asked him to point out the reference to a 'British-Irish force'.

Although the *Irish Press* pronounced the result as a draw, the general view was that FitzGerald had come out on top. 'The debate was, I think, reasonably successful from my point of view. For once I succeeded in speaking relatively slowly – and in avoiding statistics,' FitzGerald wrote in *All in a Life*.

This was echoed by John Bowman who wrote: 'What FitzGerald had in fact shown was a new willingness to accept his party strategists' advice to avoid his usual detailed statistical arguments and to accept the limitations of a televised debate of this kind.'

The next day's *Irish Independent* ran with the headline: 'Buoyant FitzGerald Wins the TV Debate'. The newspaper concluded that FitzGerald had 'put behind him the disaster' of the February performance and had shown 'a convincing demonstration of debating superiority'.

Using a boxing metaphor – perhaps FitzGerald's misgivings about the contest being perceived as pugilistic were justified – the *Independent* said: 'They changed corners, came out fighting and this time the title changed hands too.' FitzGerald had made a 'superb recovery'. 'This time he had kept his head in cool, clinical fashion. Maybe it was due to his hairdresser. For the first time in political memory, his hair was actually brushed down.'

Fine Gael strategists were annoyed the programme was allowed run over time to complete the agreed topics. 'With our man so far ahead on points after an hour, no wonder we wanted it concluded on time,' they said. The outcome of the general election mirrored the debate. Fine Gael and Labour comfortably took power and Fine Gael came within just five seats of Fianna Fáil.

Act III

The final part of the trilogy took place in February 1987. This time it was FitzGerald and Fine Gael who were on the backfoot after four very difficult years in government. Defeat in the general election a few days later seemed inevitable, despite a fairly steady decline in Fianna Fáil's opinion-poll performance. It had been agreed to open the debate with a 'harmless' question from moderator Brian Farrell before moving to the economy and then the North. FitzGerald recalled in his autobiography that whatever question Farrell asked him he became 'totally disconcerted' and lost the thread of the discussion. He was unable to follow properly the different stages of the debate. 'All I could do was keep on demanding that the leader of the opposition explain where he stood on the budgetary issue, which he had avoided throughout the campaign. After what seemed an eternity, the discussion turned to Northern Ireland,' he wrote.

On the North, FitzGerald challenged Haughey about remarks he had made concerning how renegotiating part of the Anglo-Irish Agreement of late 1985 would put at risk all that had been achieved. Haughey denied he had said that, repeatedly claiming the remarks related to emigration. FitzGerald had written the words Haughey had used on the issue and brought them into the studio but, at first, could not find them. But just as Haughey again repeated his denial, he spotted the scrap of paper and, picking it up, he proceeded to read it out. As he later recalled, he was 'unaware of the fact that a camera over my shoulder was focused on it so that the viewers could see the words themselves: "We would strive by diplomatic and political action to see if we can change these constitutional implications to which we take exception."

'It was now his turn to be disconcerted and the viewers could see that his attempt to suggest that the quotation related to emigration had been complete nonsense. The negative impact of this on his credibility was reinforced visually by the manner in which the camera had focused on the note of his words that I had read out,' FitzGerald wrote.

He added that when he emerged from the studio he found to his 'astonishment' that he was seen as the winner. 'Even my panic-driven reiteration over and over again of the demand that my opponent clarify his position on the budget had come across to viewers as a masterly tactic to put him on the spot'.

EPILOGUE

FitzGerald may have come out on top and his party's fortunes were boosted in the closing days of the campaign – the vote it got in the election was higher than any poll had recorded – but it was never going to be enough. Fine Gael duly got a hammering on polling day, losing 20 seats. However, FitzGerald's performance may possibly have been enough to deny Haughey his coveted overall majority, although the presence of the PDs was probably a bigger factor in that regard.

Haughey did succeed in forming a minority government and was Taoiseach for another four years. FitzGerald, meanwhile, resigned as party leader shortly after the general election. In the general election of 1989 Haughey refused the offer of a debate with then Fine Gael leader Alan Dukes but, that aside, TV debates have been a feature of elections since the Haughey/FitzGerald era. Generally, they have little impact on the election – for example, both John Bruton and Michael Noonan came out on top against Bertie Ahern in 1997 and 2002 respectively, but this had little or no bearing on the result. However, Ahern's performance in the debate with Enda Kenny – when he clearly got the better of an unconvincing Kenny – is regarded by many as a defining point in the 2007 general election. The fact that the debate took place a week before polling day was regarded as significant because there was more time to make an impact on voters who might not have made up their minds at that point. However, nothing will ever match the excitement of that first debate in February 1982 and the rivalry between Haughey and FitzGerald that is neatly encapsulated by an anecdote from that night.

When the two men arrived at RTÉ, they were met by *Today Tonight* presenter Barry Cowan, who asked both to autograph his clipboard on which he had typed his introductory remarks for the programme, which included the words in big letters 'Taoiseach' and 'Leader of the Opposition'. Haughey signed first, deliberately writing his name beside the word 'Taoiseach'. Garret, determined not to be outpointed before the contest even began, signed his name nearby and then drew an arrow from his signature, curving around Haughey's and pointing at 'Taoiseach'.

Despite that rivalry, after Haughey's death in 2006, FitzGerald pointed out that their relationship was 'always marked by courtesy and absence of personal antagonism' – a point illustrated by a visit to Abbeville made by FitzGerald to see an ailing Haughey in late 2005.

21

Vote Seán Phaddy Shéamus Number 1
1944

PROLOGUE

It was legendary US politician Tipp O'Neill who said that 'all politics is local', but in no Western democracy does this apply to the same extent as in Ireland. Part of it is cultural or historic and some of it is due to the PR-STV method that pitches party candidates in competition with each other – causing them to seek to outdo each other in parish-pump style politics.

Whatever the reason, the politician who focuses solely on national issues, at the expense of constituency affairs, generally finds himself or herself in difficulty at election time. In virtually every general election, at least one high-profile minister loses his or her seat. The country has become more educated, sophisticated and cosmopolitan over the past 25 years, but there has been no dilution in the clientelist nature of Irish politics.

It speaks volumes when Bertie Ahern, the man who has led the country for the previous decade and become the second longest-serving Taoiseach in the history of the state, can be seen out canvassing his constituency on a Saturday afternoon and it isn't even close to an election.

Perhaps the best illustration of the utterly local nature of Irish politics comes from the 1944 general election. As the great powers collided across Europe, the Pacific, Asia and North Africa and plunged the world into chaos, Ireland – which was neutral in the Second World War – stood isolated and remote from virtually the rest of the globe. The Emergency, as it was known, did impact on the country's citizens, in the form of censorship, rationing and so on, but nowhere near to the same extent as across the Irish Sea. Politics remained uniquely Irish.

In the summer of 1944, de Valera called a general election after his minority government was defeated in a Dáil vote. It was a bad time for the world at large, but a good time for an election for Fianna Fáil. The opposition, rarely formidable during this era, was in disarray. Fine Gael's leader Richard Mulcahy wasn't even in the Dáil, having lost his seat the previous year (see Chapter 18), while Labour had split with a breakaway National Labour Party being formed.

THE DRAMA

As ever, these national issues were only part of the election campaign, with local issues deciding many seats up and down the country, a fact of which outgoing South Kerry TD John B. Healy was obviously acutely aware. On 27 May 1944, Healy, a solicitor, placed an advert in *The Kerryman* newspaper, which purported to come from pensioner 'Seán Phaddy Shéamus'. It read:

> Just a few lines from a simple, plain countryman. I am only asking you to do what I am going to do myself next Tuesday and that is to walk six miles to the school and give my number one to John Healy. My story is not a long one. I am 76 and up to last August

was only getting seven shillings old-age pension. All because I had the grass of four cows and six or seven sheep. Over five years my case was taken up by two TDs, but I got nothing. John Healy was only six weeks in the Dáil when I got my ten shillings. He will do for any pensioner what he did for me. And pensioners, don't forget him next Tuesday.

EPILOGUE

They didn't. Healy's vote increased from 5,323 votes one year earlier to 6,526 in 1944 and he was elected on the first count, no doubt thanks to his innovative campaign strategy. During his campaign speeches, Healy had reminded his constituents that Fine Gael, in its previous incarnation as Cumann na nGaedheal, had taken a shilling off the old-age pension and that Fianna Fáil had subsequently restored that shilling.

The world may have been at war, but in Ireland the politician who could deliver the extra shilling or three to the pensioner had a head start come election time. Sixty years on, only the amounts have changed.

22

So Good they Elected him Twice
1927

PROLOGUE

There were two general elections in four months in 1927. The June election marked Fianna Fáil's first outing on the national stage and the party performed extremely well, winning 44 seats. This left Sinn Féin – the party from which it had broken away – with just five. Fianna Fáil was now within three seats of Cumann na nGaedheal's total of 47. However, de Valera's demand to enter the Dáil without taking the hated Oath of Allegiance, which involved expressing fidelity to the King of England, saw the doors of Leinster House slammed in his face.

The following month Minister for Justice and cabinet strongman, Kevin O'Higgins, was gunned down on his way to mass in Booterstown, on the southside of the capital. The President of the Executive Council – who would be known as the Taoiseach today – William T Cosgrave responded by introducing a new Public Safety Bill and, more pertinently, an Electoral Amendment Bill that required all future Dáil candidates to take the Oath. Faced with the prospect of his new party being unable to contest the next election, de Valera swallowed hard and led his party into the Dáil after coming up with his 'empty formula' solution. This involved Fianna Fáil deputies signing the book containing the Oath, but with the words covered while doing so, the Bible placed face down in the furthest corner of the room and their insistence that they were not taking any Oath. Fianna Fáil's entry into the Dáil left Cumann na nGaedheal in a minority position in the Dáil. Cosgrave's government seemed doomed to be defeated in a motion of no confidence and replaced by a Labour-led government supported by Fianna Fáil, which was not yet ready for power but very taken with the proposition of giving a bloody nose to its arch rivals.

However, overconfidence in the outcome led to one Labour TD, T J O'Connell, not being asked to return from a teachers' conference in Canada for the vote. In addition, one of the National League deputies, John Jinks, infamously went AWOL on the day. As a result, Cosgrave survived with the casting vote of the Ceann Comhairle. Later in the month Cumann na nGaedheal romped home in two by-election victories, prompting Cosgrave to call a general election for September. He was clearly seeking to take advantage of potential weaknesses in the opposition.

Labour's coffers were depleted after the June election and it must have been demoralised by snatching defeat from the jaws of victory in its August bid for power. Fianna Fáil faced the possibility of losing hard-line Republican votes after its oath-taking/empty-formula exercise, while the government's tough line on law and order after the assassination of O'Higgins would appeal to sections of the electorate who may previously have voted for independents.

22 – So Good they elected him Twice

THE DRAMA

However, not everything was rosy in the Cumann na nGaedheal garden. Posts and Telegraphs Minister and TD for Cork Borough, J J Walsh, abandoned the party and opted not to stand in the election because he was disenchanted with the government's free-trade orientation and opposition to protectionism. Cosgrave decided to fill the sizeable hole in the ticket in Cork left by Walsh by doing something that would be extraordinary in politics today, but which was actually very common in the nineteenth century. He contested the general election in both his usual constituency of Carlow–Kilkenny and in Cork Borough. (Candidates could stand for election in a number of constituencies in elections, but they could only be a member of the Dáil for one constituency.)

It says something for Cosgrave's stature that the citizens of both constituencies were clearly unconcerned that he may have been spreading himself a little thinly, as the country's leader topped the poll in both constituencies, securing around four quotas in the process. In Carlow–Kilkenny he attracted just short of 14,000 votes (almost two quotas), while he did even better in Cork Borough, getting 17,395 votes (over two quotas). His combined vote of over 31,300 votes must be the highest ever obtained by a candidate in one general election to the Dáil, although obviously it was achieved in two constituencies unlike Richard Mulcahy's record of 22,005 in one constituency. (See Chapter 10).

EPILOGUE

Cosgrave's tactic of going to the country a second time in 1927 met with only partial success. Labour did take a hiding, losing nine seats, and Cumann na nGaedheal increased its total from 47 to 62. But those gains came at the expense of its allies – farmers, independents and the National League. More worryingly, Fianna Fáil also increased its seats total from 44 to 57 and it was clear that it was only a matter of time before it would be in government. While Cosgrave once again formed a government, as J.J. Lee commented in *Ireland, 1912–1985 – Politics and Society*, 'he retreated psychologically into opposition as Fianna Fáil now stalked Cumann na nGaedheal and hunter became hunted.' This was immediately apparent in the by-election less than two months after the general election.

Because he was not capable of bi-location, not to mention the fact that the rules wouldn't allow him to represent two constituencies in the Dáil, Cosgrave opted to give up his traditional seat in Carlow-Kilkenny (presumably because that constituency was more 'winnable' in a by-election), prompting an early by-election there. There was no repeat of Cosgrave's impressive September vote, with Cumann na nGaedheal's Denis Gorey just squeaking home ahead of Fianna Fáil in a two-horse race with 50.3 per cent of the vote compared to 49.7 per cent. De Valera duly replaced Cosgrave as President of the Executive Council in 1932 after Fianna Fáil's electoral victory, but even he subsequently acknowledged the 'magnificent job' Cosgrave and his colleagues had done. In handing over the reins of power to the people he had defeated in the Civil War a decade earlier, Cosgrave also copperfastened democracy in the new state.

And just to complete his legacy, he remains the last Irish politician elected to parliament for two different constituencies. He was so good, they literally elected him twice.

23

Death on the Canvass – 2
1954

PROLOGUE

The general election of 1954 was the third of three elections in six years that failed to produce a clear-cut winner. The 1948 election resulted in the first inter-party government – a six-legged coalition made up of Fine Gael, Clann na Phoblachta, Labour, National Labour, Clann na Talmhan and independents. When it collapsed three years later resulting in a general election, de Valera formed a minority government, but that government fell in 1954 when independents withdrew their support, prompting yet another election. With the economy in the depths of depression, it was always going to be a tough election for Fianna Fáil.

THE DRAMA

It would turn out to be a vastly more difficult election for the Ledwidge family in Wicklow. Sadly, less than two weeks before polling day, Peter Ledwidge, who had been selected to contest the election for Fianna Fáil, passed away in a Dublin hospital. A War of Independence veteran and member of Fianna Fáil since its foundation, he was just 53 years old. Under the rules, proceedings in the constituency had to begin afresh and a new polling day was set for 26 May, eight days after the rest of the country voted. Ledwidge's widow, Mary, was selected to stand in his place, promising to 'keep a watching brief for the housewife' and adding that 'as my husband was a working man, I know and understand the problems which face workers'.

It must have been a surreal experience for the voters of Wicklow because it was clear for days before they voted that Fine Gael was going to form the next government. Fianna Fáil had slumped to just 64 seats – well short of a majority of 74 even if it succeeded in holding two out of three seats in Wicklow – while Fine Gael had gained four, bringing them up to 49 seats, with the strong possibility of another gain in Wicklow. A second inter-party government was inevitable and meetings were going on between Fine Gael and Labour leaders even before Wicklow voters had exercised their constitutional prerogative.

Canvassing continued in Wicklow nonetheless, with de Valera complaining that voters there were being asked to make a choice in the dark because, while the opposition could form a government, there was no policy agreed or bargains made (surely the way it was for voters in every other constituency?). He urged voters to give two out of three seats to Fianna Fáil, which could potentially have an impact on the make-up of the government.

Despite the delay, there was a 75 per cent turnout in the constituency and a mirroring of the national trend against Fianna Fáil. Fine Gael picked up a seat from Fianna Fáil's Patrick Cogan (who had been elected as an independent in 1951), leaving the three big parties with one seat apiece. After what must have been a hugely traumatic campaign for her personally, brave Mary Ledwidge came in last of the three Fianna Fáil candidates with just 2,046 votes and was eliminated on the fourth count, losing her statutory financial deposit.

EPILOGUE

Five days after the counting was completed in Wicklow, John A Costello was elected Taoiseach for the second time, forming a government with Labour and Clann na Talmhan. It had the slimmest of majorities that would be seriously undermined by three by-election defeats over the next couple of years. Costello had offered to bring Clann na Phoblachta, which had three seats, into his government, but its leader Seán MacBride declined, although it supported the government in Dáil votes.

However, MacBride withdrew his party's support for the government in 1957 over its handling of the IRA border campaign. With defeat inevitable on a motion of no confidence, Costello dissolved the Dáil and called an election for March 1957. Fianna Fáil won the election decisively, securing a comfortable overall majority and, incidentally, two out of three seats in Wicklow.

24

Bad Timing
1932 – 1997

PROLOGUE

It was the famous Canadian prime minister Pierre Trudeau who remarked that the 'essential ingredient of politics is timing'. When it comes to general elections, that is certainly the case. Irish political history is littered with examples of governments who picked the right and the wrong time to go to the country and either reaped the rewards or paid a heavy price.

THE DRAMA

Act I

In 1932, Cumann na nGaedheal had been in power for the previous ten years, but Fianna Fáil was unquestionably a major threat. The party had surprised everybody with its performances in the two general elections of 1927 and it was clearly only a matter of time before it entered government. The Cumann na nGaedheal government under William T Cosgrave had done an excellent job of putting in place the foundations for a new democratic state but, compared to Fianna Fáil, the party seemed remote, overly focused on defending the Treaty of ten years earlier at all costs, and too right wing. However, although there was an inevitability about Fianna Fáil's success, Cosgrave certainly didn't help matters by the timing of the general election. In June 1927 he had called an election at a time when agricultural prices were at their lowest levels since independence. It was only through luck, and a certain John Jinks (see Chapter 22), that he just about survived in government. But when Cumann na nGaedheal went to the country in 1932, agricultural prices were even lower. It could be argued that prices had been falling since 1930 and no time would have been particularly good for an election, but Cosgrave certainly could have waited until after the Eucharistic Congress in June of 1932 before calling an election, instead of opting for a February election. As J.J. Lee points out in *Ireland 1912–1985 – Politics and Society*, the Eucharistic Congress would have offered him the opportunity of 'being photographed incessantly with the papal nuncio for the edification of the plain people of the Free State'. It is hard to imagine Fianna Fáil missing a similar opportunity. To be fair to the government, it was – as Lee notes – at its 'wits' end' in financial matters. Its notoriously straight-laced Finance Minister, Ernest Blythe, could see no alternative to an austere budget and Cosgrave therefore decided to go to the country sooner rather than later. It would be 16 years before the party – under a new name – would gain power again.

Act II

In contrast to Cosgrave, described by Lee as 'an inept subterfugist', de Valera seemed to have a knack for picking the right moment to go to the country. In 1933, 1938 and 1944, de Valera called snap elections – in each case just a year after inconclusive general elections where Fianna Fáil failed to win an overall majority – and each time it paid off, giving his party secure majorities. In 1948, in an attempt to head off a vibrant new Clann na Phoblachta, de Valera dissolved the Dáil 18 months early. The election resulted in Fianna Fáil losing power – with a six-legged inter-party government taking over. However, in the long run, the gamble arguably paid off. Clann na Phoblachta had a disappointing election, winning just ten seats, and failed to emerge as a serious threat to Fianna Fáil.

Act III
Like 1932, the general election of 1977 was almost certainly one of those elections where the public had simply tired of the government – in this case a coalition of Fine Gael and Labour. But there were those in the cabinet who believed Taoiseach Liam Cosgrave and his Tánaiste, Labour Party leader Brendan Corish, picked the wrong time to fight the election. Garret FitzGerald, who was Foreign Affairs Minister in that government, recalled in his autobiography, *All in a Life*, that there was a strong argument for postponing the election until after the summer. The economy was starting to recover after the oil crisis and inflation was starting to come down, but it would take time for the electorate to appreciate this. 'If ever there was a case for a government remaining in office until as near as possible to the end of its term, this was it,' FitzGerald wrote. There is also the point that a government's popularity typically rises during the summer when the Dáil isn't sitting. When it came to be debated by the cabinet, FitzGerald, Finance Minister Richie Ryan and four others, mainly urban-based ministers, favoured holding on until the autumn. FitzGerald recalls that the other six ministers present favoured an immediate election, largely on the basis that if it was delayed 'something might go wrong, such as the harvest'. He put

this negativity down to a drop in morale in the government as a result of recent bad press. The casting vote fell to Cosgrave as Taoiseach with FitzGerald fairly confident that, given 'his customary caution', he would postpone a dissolution. But to FitzGerald's surprise, he decided on a June election, perhaps because it was the date that Corish wanted. Private polls commissioned by the government at the start of the election campaign proved it was the wrong decision (see Chapter 11), prompting FitzGerald to allegedly remark, on hearing the poll results, 'Can we undissolve the Dáil?' The government took a serious hiding in the election, with Fianna Fáil winning its biggest ever Dáil majority.

Act IV

If ever a Taoiseach picked the wrong time to call an election it was in 1989. Charlie Haughey and Fianna Fáil had returned to power after the 1987 general election, but only as a minority administration – a tantalising two seats short of a majority. However, the Haughey government's tough line on public spending went down a treat with voters. The party's ratings were consistently well over 50 per cent and with Fine Gael leader Alan Dukes adopting his Tallaght Strategy (supporting the government if it adhered to strict control of the public finances), it was able to survive comfortably in the Dáil. In April of 1989, however, the government was defeated in a private members' motion. Haughey should have swallowed hard, accepted the reverse – which didn't affect the stability of his government – and moved on. Instead, urged on by Pádraig Flynn and Ray Burke, he used it as an excuse to go to the country and attempt to achieve an overall majority at his fifth time of asking. It was a disastrous decision. To avoid accusations of wasting taxpayers' money, Haughey had to wait until 15 June to hold the election on the same day as the already-scheduled European elections. It certainly wasn't a 'snap election' and the opposition was well prepared. Far from winning that much-coveted majority, Fianna Fáil lost four seats after a difficult campaign dominated by health issues which the party seemed wholly unable to deal with. With just 77 seats, Fianna Fáil was in no position to form even a minority government. Haughey had to abandon the party's core value of single-party government and, traumatically for his party, he was forced to coalesce with his arch nemesis, Des O'Malley and the PDs. While in the long run it turned out to be the best thing that ever happened to Fianna Fáil – virtually guaranteeing it stayed in power – the move seriously undermined Haughey's authority. Two and a half years later, when fresh controversy emerged over the phone-tapping scandal of 1982, Haughey's fate was effectively determined by the PDs – the party that was only in government because of his decision to call an unnecessary election in 1989.

Act V

The prize for worst timing ever, though, has to go to the Rainbow Coalition. Over a decade on from the 1997 general election, Fine Gael and Labour – confined to the opposition benches ever since – must still wonder how they lost power. The Rainbow Coalition, which also included Democratic Left, had landed in power accidentally after the fall of the Fianna Fáil–Labour government in 1994. After two and a half years of good, if unspectacular, government, the Rainbow Coalition seemed to hold all the advantages going into the election year of 1997. Importantly, the economy was performing strongly. The coalition didn't need to call an election until towards the end of the year, but it opted to go to the country in June. It was a strange decision, given the traditional rise in government support during the summer months and the fact that the McCracken Tribunal was on course to finish by the summer of that year, with findings that were certain to embarrass Fianna Fáil. The belief is that Labour – anticipating major reverses after its brilliant performance in 1992 – pressurised Taoiseach John Bruton into calling the election for June, although this has been denied by Labour figures. Regardless of whose decision it was, it was almost certainly the wrong one. Fianna Fáil, helped it has to be said by Bertie Ahern's enormous personal popularity, won an election it simply had no right to win. Given the tightness of the margin, it is fair to speculate that the result might have been different had polling been deferred until September. And if ever there was an election to win, 1997 was the one. The economy was about to take off into the biggest boom in the history of the State, delivering enormous budget surpluses – and hence huge largesse to distribute – to whichever party was in power. Fianna Fáil seized the opportunity that the Rainbow Coalition handed it in 1997 and didn't look back, winning the next two general elections in 2002 and 2007.

EPILOGUE

Having watched at close quarters Charlie Haughey's mistake in 1989 and having been the beneficiary of the Rainbow coalition's decision to go for a summer election in 1997, Bertie Ahern has clearly learned from the mistakes of others. He has deliberately allowed both his governments to go their full terms, reasoning that unlike in the time of de Valera, the politically apathetic public won't thank a government for an early election.

And having won his third term in a row as Taoiseach, it's hard to argue with his logic . . . or his timing.

25

I Deem the Candidate ... Bankrupt
1927

PROLOGUE

Leinster House, no more than any other parliament, has had its share of rogues over the years. Although the election of certain politicians has horrified sections of the public, the essence of democracy is that the final word is left to the voters. Sometimes, however, this is not the case. One factor is guaranteed to disbar a politician from the Dáil, regardless of the will of the electorate: being an undischarged bankrupt. It happened to one of the best-known figures in twentieth-century Ireland. Jim Larkin was an iconic, but deeply divisive figure in the Irish trade union movement.

During a colourful career, he transformed the lives of working people, establishing both the ITGWU and the WUI (which have since merged to become SIPTU), helping to found the Irish Labour Party, and becoming a member of the Soviet Union's Comintern Executive. He is best known for his role in the Great Dublin Lock-out of 1913, when the workers were faced down by their employers in a bitter eight-month dispute.

After returning from the US in 1923, where he had been imprisoned during the 'Red Scare' of 1920, Larkin fell out with William O'Brien who had greatly developed the ITGWU in

Larkin's absence. Larkin left to found the WUI. He also established the pro-Soviet Union and pro-communist Irish Workers' League (IWL). Larkin was deeply critical of the Cumann na nGaedheal government, whilst also conducting a campaign of vilification against his former (and future) colleagues in what he called the 'God-Save-the-King' Irish Labour Party and against other figures in the wider labour movement. In May 1924, an article in Larkin's newspaper, the *Irish Worker*, launched a serious and unfair diatribe against Thomas Johnson, the leader of the Labour Party in the Dáil.

Johnson had recently made a Dáil speech calling for unemployment to be dealt with as in a war. This was ridiculously misconstrued in the article in the *Irish Worker* (though not actually written by Larkin) as 'incitement to murder the workers' by the 'English traitor' (like Larkin, Johnson was born in Liverpool). Johnson sued both Larkin and the printers of the newspaper for £1,000 each in damages. Not surprisingly, he won the libel action the following year and the court awarded £500 damages against both Larkin and the printers. Larkin refused to pay. He had also built up costs, which he refused to settle as a matter of principle, in a unsuccessful legal action he had taken against the executive of the ITGWU. Because of his failure to settle his outstanding legal costs, Larkin was declared bankrupt. The timing of this bankruptcy would prove to be particularly unfortunate.

THE DRAMA

Larkin's Irish Workers' League contested the general election of September 1927. The Labour Party was demoralised after coming so close to defeating Cumann na nGaedheal in the Dáil and

25 – I Deem the Candidate... Bankrupt

forming a government of its own just weeks beforehand, so it was a good time to take it on. Despite its fringe status and its labelling as a party of 'communists' in the media, IWL duly outpolled Labour in three Dublin constituencies. Larkin was elected in Dublin North on the third count with an impressive 7,490 votes. His son James Jnr failed to win a seat in County Dublin, but it wasn't all bad news there. By splitting the Labour vote, he had denied Thomas Johnson the seat – some measure of revenge for the libel action. A third IWL candidate ended any chance of a Labour seat in South Dublin.

However, because of his bankruptcy status, Larkin could not take his seat in the Dáil. Even if he had not been bankrupt, the existence of the Oath of Allegiance may well have proved another obstacle, according to one of his biographers, R.M. Fox.

EPILOGUE

Larkin's seat was declared vacant and a by-election called for April 1928. Larkin contested the by-election along with Fianna Fáil and Cumann na nGaedheal. However, he came in a poor third, and the government candidate took the seat with almost three times Larkin's vote. According to Emmet Larkin, another of his biographers, Jim Larkin was very bitter that Fianna Fáil had contested the seat. Given that he had urged first-preference votes for Fianna Fáil in other constituencies in the September general election, he had hoped that the party would opt out of the by-election, leaving it as a straight fight between him and Cumann na nGaedheal (he obviously didn't know Fianna Fáil!).

However, he later said that he was glad Fianna Fáil had done what it had done because 'it showed that the workers had to have their own party and their own movement'. Ironically, it was his presence in the by-election that probably cost Fianna Fáil the seat.

The indefatigable Larkin did ultimately get to sit in Dáil Éireann, however. He was elected to the ninth Dáil for Dublin North-East in 1937 as an independent Labour candidate, defeating no less a politician than General Richard Mulcahy (see Chapter 10) for the final seat. By this stage he had made arrangements to satisfy his creditors and was no longer a bankrupt. Unfortunately, he was the victim of de Valera's decision to hold a snap election a year later and lost out to Mulcahy in the re-match. Three years later he and James Jnr had joined the Labour Party and, in 1943, he was returned to the Dáil, again defeating Mulcahy (who after this defeat decamped to contest future elections in Tipperary). Once again, Larkin's luck was out, and when de Valera called a snap election a year later, he failed to hold the seat. It was to be the last election 'Big Jim' would contest.

Eighty years after he was prevented from taking his seat, the constitutionality of the legislation disbarring a bankrupt person from membership of Dáil Éireann was about to be tested by another elected politician, Beverley Flynn. Flynn had taken the action after being served with a bankruptcy petition by RTÉ, days after being re-elected to the Dáil in 2007. However, the constitutional challenge did not go ahead because Flynn reached a settlement with RTÉ on the costs of her failed libel action against the broadcaster, meaning the bankruptcy proceedings were adjourned. Whether the bankruptcy provision in the Electoral Act would have stood up to the scrutiny of the courts is, for now at least, just a matter for speculation.

26

A Bad Day for Fine Gael
2002

PROLOGUE

The years 1997 to 2002 were not good ones to be in opposition. The country was going through the greatest boom in the history of the State – there was full employment, wealth was increasing and spending power had strengthened accordingly. The feel-good factor was enormous. What was particularly galling for Fine Gael was that it had been in government for two and a half years leading up to June 1997. Fine Gael members knew that they could have been enjoying the fruits of that boom instead of Fianna Fáil and the PDs. The party had narrowly lost the 1997 election, which it probably should have won, given the general view that the Rainbow coalition government of Fine Gael, Labour and Democratic Left had done a decent job in office. The enormous personal popularity of Bertie Ahern, a collapse in support for Labour from its high of 1992 and an unwise decision to hold the election in June cost the Rainbow coalition that election (see Chapter 24).

Despite a series of scandals emerging from the tribunals, the opinion polls showed that Fine Gael in opposition were not impressing the public, with the party languishing at around 20 per cent and the satisfaction rating of former Taoiseach John Bruton falling. By early 2001, Fine Gael TDs were so alarmed at the party's slide that they took the drastic – and disastrous – step of voting no confidence in Bruton. He was replaced by the supposed dream-team of Michael Noonan and Jim Mitchell. But it was quickly apparent that the change in leadership had done nothing to improve the electorate's perception of Fine Gael.

It was also obvious that the public was not warming to Noonan – a highly capable politician, but one who, as Stephen Collins recalled in *People, Politics and Power – From O'Connell to Ahern*, conveyed 'a harsh and uncompromising image by comparison with the wily Ahern'. Noonan's handling of the Hepatitis C controversy, while Minister for Health in the Rainbow government, came back to haunt his leadership and allowed opposing political parties and the media to present him very unfairly as heartless. The problem was compounded by an RTÉ television drama on the Hepatitis C issue – *No Tears* – broadcast in early 2002, which unfavourably represented his actions while he was Minister for Health. It was clear, heading into the 2002 election, that Fine Gael was in trouble and Fianna Fáil was heading back to power – the only question was with which party, if any. Private polls showed Fine Gael in meltdown and the party did not help its cause with a series of ill-considered policy measures, including a proposal to compensate Eircom shareholders who had lost money buying shares in the flotation of the former semi-state company and taxi drivers adversely affected by the deregulation of the market.

The party's election manifesto lacked credibility, with a range of goodies that most people believed were not deliverable. With that manifesto, the party lost its chance to tackle the government on a clear weak spot, the state of the public finances after some fairly profligate spending by Fianna Fáil and the PDs in the two years leading up to the election. Throw into the mix less-than-catchy slogans, such as 'I'll legislate for Social Justice', and it was clear that the party was in free-fall. Disastrously for Fine Gael, Labour decided to keep its coalition options open and there was a perception that there was no alternative to a Fianna Fáil-led government. Fine Gael had become irrelevant to the outcome of the general election. Even so, nobody expected the wipe-out that was to follow.

THE DRAMA

It's not unusual for elections to throw up shocks and for big names to lose their seats, particularly in Ireland given the strong local emphasis in elections. However, what happened to Fine Gael in 2002 was unprecedented. It wasn't just that the party lost 23 of its 54 seats, it was the quality of the TDs that lost their seats. The front bench of the party was virtually wiped out.

The casualty list included former leader Alan Dukes (one of the finest politicians of his or any generation); deputy leader and former cabinet minister Jim Mitchell; former deputy leader and former Justice Minister Nora Owen (see Chapter 3); former presidential candidate Austin Currie; the daughter of former deputy leader Peter Barry, Deirdre Clune; senior party figures such as Alan Shatter, Frances Fitzgerald and Jim Higgins (it could just as easily have been Enda Kenny, who was just 87 votes ahead when Higgins was eliminated); and some of the party's brightest young talent: Paul Bradford, Brian Hayes, Charlie Flanagan and Gerry Reynolds.

In Dún Laoghaire, once its stronghold, where it held three seats, it amazingly failed to return even one TD. And in Dublin generally, where Garret FitzGerald had lorded it over Fianna Fáil 20 years earlier, the party came in fifth place – behind Fianna Fáil, Labour, the Greens and the PDs – winning a miserable three seats.

EPILOGUE

After less than 18 months in the job, Michael Noonan took the only option open to him after the election disaster, resigning on the day of the count. It was no wonder that some commentators were questioning whether Fine Gael had a future at all. By the time of the next general election, it was going to be 25 years since the party had won an election. At fifty seats behind Fianna Fáil, winning the 2007 election looked an impossibility. In the ensuing leadership contest, Enda Kenny defeated Richard Bruton to become party leader. Seriously underestimated, he set about rebuilding his shattered party.

While many felt the job was beyond him, he surprised everybody by revitalising Fine Gael and, with the help of the Mullingar Accord alliance with Pat Rabbitte's Labour, making them credible contenders in the 2007 general election. However, it was always going to take more than one election to bridge the gap caused by Fine Gael's 2002 disaster. Although Fine Gael gained close to 20 seats, the party's efforts to return to government ultimately fell short after support swung back to Fianna Fáil in the final week of the 2007 campaign.

27

The Electorally Embarrassed 1923

PROLOGUE

There is no set number of votes that can guarantee a candidate will be elected to Dáil Éireann. Everything depends on the constituency, the size of the electorate in the constituency, the quota and the number of votes received by rivals. There are examples of candidates failing to get elected in one general election and then winning a seat next time around, despite receiving a couple of thousand less votes.

In the 2002 general election, former Tánaiste Dick Spring failed to get elected in Kerry North, despite polling almost 9,000 first-preference votes, thousands more than many successful candidates had received in other constituencies. In the 2007 general election, Cyprian Brady was elected in Dublin Central despite only receiving 939 first-preference votes, 13% of the vote received by Ivor Callely in adjoining Dublin North-Central who failed to be elected. However, Brady's first-preference vote is not the lowest ever received by a successful Dáil candidate. For that record, we have to go back to the general election of August 1923.

27 – The Electorally Embarrassed

THE DRAMA

The general election of 1923 took place just after the bitter Civil War, and the anti-Treaty Republicans ran a number of candidates in the five-seat constituency of Clare (see Chapter 39). Its clear frontrunner, however, was Éamon de Valera, the leading politician on the anti-Treaty side, who had been elected unopposed for the constituency in the previous three Dáil elections. He was joined on the Sinn Féin ticket by TD Brian O'Higgins, who had also been elected unopposed in the same three elections, and Frank Barrett. Not surprisingly, de Valera topped the poll with an enormous 17,762 votes – more than twice his Cumann na nGaedheal rival, Professor Eoin MacNeill, and almost three times the quota. Barrett polled just 482 first-preference votes, while O'Higgins fared even worse with just 114.

However, de Valera's surplus was so large that it was inevitable he would elect one of his running mates. His transfers favoured O'Higgins, who took part in the 1916 Rising, and was responsible for seeing that the Sinn Féin or Republican courts were first attempted in his original West Clare constituency (these courts were established as an alternative to the British legal system and were widely used). O'Higgins got more than 4,900 of de Valera's transfers, compared to just over 1,900 for Barrett, propelling him from bottom of the heap to well ahead of those candidates contesting the remaining three seats. When Barrett was finally eliminated, his transfers elected Higgins on the twelfth count. Higgins ended up with 7,943 votes, 69 times more than he got in first-preference votes, thanks to the blessings of PR-STV.

EPILOGUE

O'Higgins has an incredible record in that he was elected to the first four Dála, only securing 114 first-preference votes in the process. In the first three general elections he was, like many SF candidates, returned unopposed, and it was in the fourth that he received the raft of transfers from de Valera. In that 1923 election, he lay joint last of the 15 candidates after the first count; the other candidate, who also received 114 votes, actually lost his statutory financial deposit. Patrick MacNamara of the Labour Party received 20 times more first-preference votes than O'Higgins in that election in the same constituency and failed to be elected, highlighting the weird and wonderful workings of the PR-STV electoral system.

O'Higgins, like the other Republican candidates in that election, including de Valera, did not take his seat in the fourth Dáil. Three years later, although he had been elected on the back of de Valera's transfers, the uncompromising Republican did not follow his constituency colleague by leaving Sinn Féin and joining the new Fianna Fáil party. In the general election of June 1927, he stood in Clare as a Sinn Féin candidate. Although on this occasion he increased his vote more than tenfold to over 1,400, he failed to be elected.

He went on to become President of Sinn Féin between 1931–33. He was editor of the *Wolfe Tone Annual* and became well known for songwriting and poetry and his Celtic greeting cards, which can still be purchased on eBay.

O'Higgins was not the only person elected to the Dáil on a rather small mandate. The two constituencies of Dublin University and National University of Ireland – which since the 1937 election have been part of the Seanad (but before that elected six TDs between them) – had extremely small electorates and were the new Irish state's equivalent of the rotten boroughs (see Chapter 43) that used to be so common in British elections. In the same 1923 general election as O'Higgins was elected with just 114 first-preference votes, Professor William Magennis was elected with just 201 first-preference votes for the National University constituency. The poll-topper, with a less than enormous total of 418, was Cumann na nGaedheal Professor Eoin MacNeill, who was also elected for Clare in the same general election (standing in more than one constituency was not particularly unusual then and had been quite common in the nineteenth century).

Over in the Dublin University constituency, James Craig was returned to the Dáil in seven consecutive elections. In six of these, he was returned unopposed; in the other he was elected second with just 356 first-preference votes.

Just for the record, the lowest vote ever received by an individual in a general election was in Dublin North-West in 1997, when a candidate received an unlucky 13 votes. Needless to say the candidate in question was not elected.

28

The 21 Lost Deputies
1923 – 1927

PROLOGUE

As in any Western liberal democracy, by-elections are a regular, though not particularly frequent, occurrence in the lifetime of any Dáil. They occur when a TD dies, resigns his or her seat or, much more rarely, when a deputy is disqualified from the Dáil for reasons of bankruptcy or a prison term exceeding six months. In the past, by-elections have played crucial roles in Irish political history. For example, the loss of two by-elections by Fianna Fáil in 1979 effectively pushed Jack Lynch into resigning as party leader and Taoiseach. However, over the last 25 years they have become much more predictable, with a trend emerging whereby the government of the day always loses a by-election, even if it is defending one of its own seats. Thus, they are no longer seen as a good measure of what may happen in the ensuing general election. During Bertie Ahern's tenure as Taoiseach, Fianna Fáil has performed badly and lost every by-election the party has contested, yet the party has twice been returned to government by the electorate at general election time, on each occasion winning back any seat it had previously held but lost in a by-election. Obviously the number of by-elections varies from Dáil to Dáil. The last three Dála have each run their full term: the twenty-seventh Dáil had seven by-elections (four of which were caused by deaths); the twenty-eighth had six (five deaths) and the twenty-ninth just two (happily, no deaths). But when it comes to by-elections there is one Dáil that stands out – the fourth Dáil between 1923 and 1927. A total of 21 TDs – or almost one in seven of the deputies – either resigned their seats, were disqualified or died during its four years. On one single day, halfway through its term, eight seats were filled in by-elections.

THE DRAMA

Only four of the 21 seats made vacant were caused by death. Of the rest, one was caused by the appointment of Attorney General Hugh Kennedy as Chief Justice – Kennedy had been elected to the Dáil in a by-election only a year earlier! A second was caused by a TD retiring after he was made Film Censor. Two TDs were disqualified after being sent to prison (see Chapter 9). Two of the by-elections were caused by the practice of high-profile figures contesting more than one constituency in the general election and then standing down from the seat deemed to be most easily won in a by-election (this practice continued right through the 1920s, including the September 1927 general election when William T Cosgrave stood in two constituencies – see Chapter 22). The remaining eleven were caused by resignation, eight of which can be put down to the fallout from the army mutiny. The Minister for Industry, Joe McGrath, resigned from the cabinet in protest at the government's handling of the affair and brought together an eight-strong 'National Group' of similarly minded Cumann na nGaedheal TDs. They put down a series of conditions for their support of the government. When this was rejected by the cabinet

– Cosgrave had been amenable - the National Group resigned their seats on 30 October 1924.

It was a potentially shattering blow for the government to lose so many of its supporters in one move. But there was to be no windfall for de Valera's Republicans – the government won six of the eight seats the following March. The only Republican successes came in the two constituencies where there were two resignations and therefore two seats being contested. Even in those two constituencies, Cumann na nGaedheal topped the poll. Indeed, of the 21 seats contested in the Dáil, the government party won all bar five – losing just four seats it had initially held and picking up a gain in Laois-Offaly, the exact opposite of what happens today, when governments always fail to win by-elections.

EPILOGUE

While the fourth Dáil lost a big name in Joe McGrath, who would go on to be very successful in business and later supportive of Fine Gael, it gained a future Taoiseach in one of the by-elections. Hugh Kennedy's seat in Dublin South was taken by Republican candidate Seán Lemass in November 1924. Just to complete the turmoil of that Dáil, in late 1925 three Cumann na nGaedheal TDs resigned from their party, though not the Dáil, in the wake of the Boundary Agreement that left the border between North and South unchanged. The three accused their party of accepting partition and established Clann Éireann. However, the party had no electoral success, and most of its members later joined Fianna Fáil.

All in all, though, it was a fairly hectic four years. They simply don't make Dála like that any more.

29

It's a Long Count in Tipperary
1943

PROLOGUE

The tenth Dáil was dissolved in the summer of 1943 with a general election called for 23 June. Unusually, the Dáil had served its full term, lasting just short of five years. The time between the 1938 and 1943 general elections, five years and six days, was a record for the State that lasted until 2007, when the electorate had to wait for five years and seven days from May 2002 to cast its vote in a general election.

1943 was also the year that de Valera made his famous and much derided (unfairly so) St Patrick's Day radio broadcast that dreamed of an Ireland of 'sturdy children', 'athletic youth' and 'comely maidens' who valued material wealth only as the basis of the right way to live. The rest of the world was at war, but the neutral Irish State was less affected than many others. Given international events, there were calls (including, not surprisingly, from Fine Gael) for a national government (i.e. a government made up of all parties) but Fianna Fáil resisted these. Besides, in effect, the country already had a national governnment – a Fianna Fáil national government. The 1943 general election returned the party to power for a fifth successive time.

THE DRAMA

It was a largely uneventful election, but it does contain one notable historical footnote – the marathon count in the constituency of Tipperary, which could only happen with our unusual electoral system. There have been counts in certain constituencies since then (see Chapters 13 and 14) that have taken longer because of candidates disputing both votes and outcomes in a particularly tight contest, but the 21-stage count needed to elect seven TDs (seven-seat constituencies were quite normal in those days) in Tipp is surely some sort of record. The primary reason for the 21-stage count was the presence of 24 candidates in the field, allowing voters under STV-PR to express their preference for all 24 would-be TDs if they so wished.

With the exception of legendary War of Independence hero Dan Breen, who was elected on the first count, the vote was remarkably well spread across all candidates, with only two of the 24 failing to secure at least 1,200 votes. Fifteen candidates had over 2,000 votes. After Breen's election, it would take another 15 counts before a second candidate would be deemed elected – Fine Gael's Dan Morrissey, the man Dan Breen had rescued from the clutches of Ernie O'Malley in 1922 (see Chapter 5). By the nineteenth count – if anyone still cared at that point – Fianna Fáil had two more candidates elected. And at the end of the . . . *groan* . . . twenty-first count, three more candidates were deemed elected, two of whom had not reached the quota.

Surprisingly, given the number of counts, the final result was not particularly tight, with the unlucky, and no doubt exhausted, candidate in eighth position – some 1,200 votes behind William O'Donnell of Clann na Talmhan (meaning 'family of the land') –

29 – It's a Long Count in Tipperary

taking the last seat. But the unluckiest people of all must have been those employed to do the counting. And it didn't get much easier as the counts went on. In the final count, for example, the enumerators still had nearly 5,000 votes to distribute.

EPILOGUE

The 21-stage count brought little joy to the two main parties, with Fianna Fáil and Fine Gael both losing a seat apiece and losing over 13 per cent of their vote in the constituency from the 1938 election. The beneficiaries were Labour and Clann na Talmhan and the final result was three Fianna Fáil, two Fine Gael, one Labour and one Clann an Talmhan. Nationally, Fianna Fáil had a poor enough election despite its plea to the electorate 'not to change horses mid-stream', with its vote dropping by 10 per cent.

However, Fine Gael's share of the vote dropped even more – as in Tipperary, Labour and Clann na Talmhan were the beneficiaries. The opposition was fragmented and Fianna Fáil were able to continue in office with a minority government. Less than a year later, de Valera did what he had successfully done twice before and went to the country early, after a Dáil defeat. As in 1933 and 1938, the gamble paid off, giving Fianna Fáil 76 seats and a thumping majority. One of those seats was in Tipperary. Happily, though, for those counting the votes, the field was reduced to a more manageable 13 (clearly lucky for some) candidates.

30

Election? What Election?
1920

PROLOGUE

Irish general elections are renowned for being closely fought contests. Whereas in Britian the first-past-the-post voting system and single-member constituencies mean that a 40 per cent vote for a party can result in a sweeping overall majority, our electoral system generally results in a tight contest. Inevitably, the make-up of a government is determined by a couple of hundred votes scattered across a few constituencies. But not in every case.

In fact, one Dáil election actually holds a record in Western democracy for its total absence of competition. In 1920, the British government, in the ultimate too-little-too-late gesture, introduced its Government of Ireland Act, which saw the establishment of a government and parliament in both Northern and Southern Ireland. By this stage the first Dáil had already convened in the Mansion House as the 73 Sinn Féiners elected to the House of Commons in 1918 didn't take their seats at Westminster, instead opting to set up an alternative Irish parliament in January 1919.

The elections for the two new Irish parliaments came at the height of the War of Independence in May 1921. In the North, the Unionists, setting a familiar pattern for the next half a century or so, won 40 out of the 52 seats. The remaining 12 seats there were divided evenly between Sinn Féin (with de Valera, Arthur Griffiths and Collins taking seats) and the old Nationalist Party. But if that seemed like a no-contest for the Unionists, it was nothing compared to what happened in the South.

THE DRAMA

Incredibly by today's standards, but perhaps not surprisingly given there was a war going on, all 128 seats in the new parliament were filled without a contest. Sinn Féin simply nominated the relevant number of candidates to fill all the seats in the constituencies. Those candidates were returned unopposed, leaving the party with 124 seats.

John Dillon, the last leader of the by-then irrelevant Irish Parliamentary Party, complained that the repressive policy of the British government made it impossible for a nationalist Irishman to fight Sinn Féin. The remaining four seats were filled by Unionists, representing Trinity College. They too were returned unopposed, making it the only election ever in a Western democracy where every single seat was uncontested.

EPILOGUE

While the Northern Parliament was officially opened by King George V (Sinn Féin and the Nationalists stayed away), the Southern Parliament was effectively stillborn. The 124 Sinn Féin members continued to meet separately, using the title the Second Dáil. In his comprehensive work, *Irish Elections, 1918–77*, Cornelius O'Leary records that for the initial session of the

Parliament of Southern Ireland in June 1921, only the four Unionist Trinity representatives turned up, which must have made for an interesting debate. At the second meeting, only two of them attended; the other two presumably realising they had better things to do with their time than appearing in a political version of *Hamlet* without the prince.

Within months a truce had been agreed in the War of Independence and, under the ensuing Treaty, O'Leary notes, the parliament of Southern Ireland was resurrected. The provisional government was made responsible to the parliament and sessions were constituted by the 60 pro-Treaty TDs and the four Trinity deputies. Future elections, however, were about to get a lot more competitive – thankfully.

31

The TDs Behind the Wire
1981

PROLOGUE

1981 was a particularly tense time, both in Northern Ireland and south of the border. In March of that year IRA prisoners in Long Kesh, *aka* the H Blocks, tried to re-establish their political status in the prison – removed five years earlier – by resuming a hunger strike that had finished at the end of 1980. The second hunger strike struggled initially to generate popular support, but that changed dramatically when one of the hunger strikers, Bobby Sands, was put forward to contest the Fermanagh–South Tyrone by-election.

Sands was famously elected to the British House of Commons in April, but died the following month. By this stage the world's media had descended on Northern Ireland. Feelings were running extremely high and the hunger strikers now had huge public sympathy, north and south of the border, well beyond the core Republican support. Charlie Haughey's Fianna Fáil government made major efforts to try and bring an end to the hunger strikes, but to no avail. The prisoners' action actually caused Haughey to defer his plans for a general election, which was finally called for 11 June 1981. It is widely believed an earlier election would have suited Fianna Fáil better. Haughey initially planned to call an election in February, but the tragic Stardust fire, which killed 48 young people, caused the party's Ard Fheis and election plans to be postponed. Fianna Fáil enjoyed a big lead in the campaign's early opinion polls, but an imaginative tax-cutting manifesto put forward by Garret FitzGerald's Fine Gael helped cut into his lead. To make matters worse for Haughey, buoyed by its success in Fermanagh–South Tyrone, the Republican movement decided, after much deliberation, to run nine prisoners in selected constituencies in the general election to raise the profile of the hunger strike further.

THE DRAMA

The H-Block candidates stunned everybody by their performance. Dundalk-man Paddy Agnew topped the poll in Louth, while Ciaran Doherty got more than 9,000 votes in Cavan–Monaghan to take a seat. In Sligo–Leitrim Joe McDonnell came close to winning a seat, and the candidates averaged 10.2 per cent of the vote in the constituencies they contested. Both Doherty and McDonnell died within weeks of polling day. Agnew, who was not on hunger strike, later recalled that he heard the news of his election from one of his fellow prisoners shouting across to his wing: 'That effort [Agnew] has just topped the poll.' Their success was disastrous for Fianna Fáil. The party would certainly have won an extra seat in Louth and Cavan–Monaghan without the H-Block candidates, while it was probably also denied a third seat in Sligo–Leitrim by McDonnell's strong performance. These setbacks proved crucial in what was a particularly tight election. Fianna Fáil ended up with 78 seats compared to Fine Gael and Labour's combined total of 80. Garret FitzGerald was elected

Taoiseach with the support of three independents, but the outcome would have been different if Fianna Fáil had won those two or three extra seats. Given that Fianna Fáil could also be certain of the vote of independent Fianna Fáil TD Neil Blaney, Haughey rather than FitzGerald would have been in the driving seat.

EPILOGUE

Although one of the intentions of running candidates was to increase pressure on the Irish and British governments to resolve the prisoner issue, the election of Sands in the North and Agnew and Doherty in the South ended up having a much wider significance. It was a major turning point for the Republican movement, pointing the way to an alternative electoral strategy. Although standing as 'the H-block candidates', these were Sinn Féin's first electoral successes in the South since the general election of 1957 when, at the height of the IRA border campaign, it had four TDs elected. It would be a long time before the Republican movement abandoned its twin strategy of 'ballot box in one hand and Armalite in the other', but the success in Fermanagh–South Tyrone (Owen Carron held the seat for Sinn Féin later in the summer after Sands' death) and in the 1981 general election showed Republicans the possibilities that lay ahead.

However, there was also a sense of what might have been if the H-Block or Sinn Féin candidates had been able to take their seats in the Dáil, given the tightness of the election. In his definitive work, *A Secret History of the IRA*, Ed Moloney describes it as 'a missed opportunity'. He wrote that before nominating the nine prisoners there had been divisions on the National H-Blocks

Committee. Some wanted to run non-prisoner candidates who would take their seats in the Dáil, on the grounds that they might be able to hold the balance of power. However, there were no guarantees this would be the case and the Sinn Féin leadership vetoed the idea – it would be another few years before the movement was ready to abandon its absentionist policy. But Moloney notes that 'had Doherty and Agnew been able to take their Dáil seats, or if non-prisoner candidates had run, the pro-hunger striker candidates would have held the balance of power and the history of the prison protest and much subsequent Anglo-Irish history might well have been very different'.

However, given the IRA's campaign of violence and the resultant public perception of Sinn Féin as being very 'outside the pale', it is difficult to believe that any of the mainstream political parties would have been willing to deal with pro-hunger strike candidates openly, regardless of the numbers in Dáil Éireann. Sinn Féin did contest the following February's general election but, with the hunger strikes over, the popular support dissipated; it won less than half the votes it had eight months earlier and failed to win any seats. The party did not contest the November 1982 general election in the Republic.

Although it continued to make electoral gains in the North, it would be another 15 years before it made another Dáil breakthrough with Caoimhghín Ó Caoláin winning a seat in Doherty's constituency of Cavan–Monaghan. Five years later, in 2002, it added four more seats, including one in Louth. When the election of Arthur Morgan was announced, the man hoisting Morgan aloft on his shoulder was none other than Paddy Agnew.

32

The Gerrymanders
1930 – 1974

PROLOGUE

With changes and shifts in the population guaranteed to occur, constituencies need to be revised regularly. Since the early 1980s, such revisions have been carried out by an independent boundary commission. However, before that change, such revisions were the prerogative of the Minister for Local Government (now known as the Minister for Enviroment, Heritage and Local Government). While the Minister was constrained by constitutional requirements to maintain a relatively equal TD to population ratio across the constituencies, imaginative redrawing of the electoral boundaries could be used to give the governing party an advantage in the next general election. Political parties were not shy about using this power.

THE DRAMA

Act I
In 1930, the Cumann na nGaedheal government looked at a possible revision of the constituencies but, conscious of the

enormous challenge it would face from Fianna Fáil in the next general election, the executive council (cabinet) postponed a decision 'pending further examination of the relevant figures' – political speak for putting it on the long finger – before finally deciding not to make any changes.

Act II

When Fianna Fáil won the 1932 general election, it quickly decided to examine the issue. By the following year, a cabinet subcommittee, including the President of the Executive Council, Éamon de Valera, was established, and a year later the cabinet approved the redistribution of seats. According to J.J. Lee in *Ireland 1912–1985*, 'the committee performed the operation with surgical skill.' It reduced the number of seats from 153 to 138, transferring the six university seats – from the Trinity College and National University of Ireland constituencies – to the Seanad.

It was an obvious move for the government. The best Fianna Fáil could ever hope for from those six seats would be two TDs from the National University. Trinity College/Dublin University was guaranteed to return three unionist TDs, who would support Cumann na nGaedheal. That said, the logic for scrapping such obviously elitist constituencies in a modern democracy could hardly be debated; in Trinity the candidates were generally returned unopposed, while in the 1923 general election a TD was returned from the National University constituency with just 201 first-preference votes (the poll topper had just 418). The revision worked well for Fianna Fáil. Over the next four general elections, it got an average of 6.5 additional seats than its vote entitled it to on strict proportionality grounds. In contrast, Cumann na nGaedheal's successor, Fine Gael, averaged a gain of 0.25 per cent seats.

Lee summed it up perfectly when he said: 'The deliberations of the cabinet committee of 1933 contributed powerfully to the electoral stability of the following decade!'

Act III

The next time Fianna Fáil looked at the constituencies was in 1942, when its fortunes seemed to be on the wane. However, the constitutional requirement for equality of representation was something of a problem. The government wasn't impressed with the Department of Local Government's finding that Dublin was underrepresented (with one TD per 25,000 people) compared to the rest of the country (one TD per 20,700 people). Given Labour's strength and Fianna Fáil's relative weakness in the capital, it was not surprising that the issue was postponed until after the 1943 election, especially as the party was under no constitutional obligation to change the constituencies until 1947.

With that election confirming the dangers for Fianna Fáil of shifting the balance of TDs in favour of Dublin (the party got a seat bonus of nine with the system weighted more towards rural areas), nothing more was done until after the 1944 election. However, the following year, with the deliberations of a cabinet subcommittee on the issue about to be completed, the June presidential election caused a serious rethink. While Sean T O'Kelly won the election for Fianna Fáil, he did not win a majority of the vote and, worse, the transfers of a Republican candidate went more than 4:1 to Fine Gael's Sean MacEoin rather than to O'Kelly. 'Constituency revision had to be looked at again,' wrote J.J. Lee.

Ignoring opposition demands for an all-party committee on constituency revision to prevent what Labour described as 'hoofling', Local Government Minister Séan MacEntee continued his deliberations. But there had to be yet another shift in thinking in early 1946 with the formation of a new party, Clann na Poblachta, which would seriously threaten Fianna Fáil's Republican constituency. The long-drawn-out saga finally came to a close in October 1947 with a new Electoral (Amendment) Bill.

The revision was clearly aimed at Clann na Poblachta, with an increase in the number of three-seat constituencies that favoured bigger parties and a surprising increase in the number of TDs. As the *Irish Independent* pointed out, 12 years earlier Fianna Fáil had decided to reduce the number of TDs to 138 but now, despite a falling population, the number of TDs was raised to the maximum of 147 under the new constitution. The Department of Local Government stretched credibility somewhat when it justified the increase on the basis that a significant amount of temporary emigration had taken place between 1939 and 1946 and this 'temporary phenomenon, which should be offset by a reverse trend in the next few years, has been taken into account in the fixing of the future membership of Dáil Éireann'. J.J. Lee summed it up nicely when he said that, given emigration was rising and the economic situation was disastrous, 'it must qualify as one of the most delicious pieces of fiction ever devised by even a harassed electoral cartographer to frustrate the will of the people.'

De Valera went to the country in February 1948 – 15 months early – to head off the rise of Clann na Poblachta. Despite a decent first-preference vote, though not as big as expected, Clann na Poblachta won just ten seats. While there were a number of reasons for this poor return, MacEntee's constituency revision was certainly key, with Lee noting that it would have won 19 seats had it secured representation proportional to its vote. But he also added that the Fianna Fáil obsession with the new party helped Fine Gael, which had been in serious decline since 1932. While

Fine Gael did not have a particularly good election, its ratio of seats to votes was close to Fianna Fáil's and twice as high as Clann na Poblachta's. Lee suggests that if Fianna Fáil had 'concentrated in the constituency revision on driving further nails into Fine Gael's coffin, it might have succeeded in reducing its number of seats below a credible minimum'. So while the revision arguably cut off the rise of a new rival, it may have breathed new life into Fianna Fáil's more traditional foe which went from strength to strength in the following few years. Nor did the constituency revision keep Fianna Fáil in power – although the reasons for loss of office lay elsewhere – as to everyone's surprise, all five opposition parties, along with independents, combined to form the State's first inter-party government.

Act IV

In the late 1960s, the then Fianna Fáil Minister for Local Government Kevin Boland conducted a surgical constituency revision. Boland's strategy was straightforward. He opted for three-seat constituencies in areas where Fianna Fáil was strong – on the basis that it had a good chance of winning two out of three seats – and four-seaters in Dublin, allowing Fianna Fáil a chance of taking two out of four seats despite having only a minority of the vote.

There is no question that the revision helped Fianna Fáil in the 1969 general election, as the party managed to win 52 per cent of the Dáil's seats with 45.7 per cent of the vote. This was virtually an unprecedented seat bonus by the standards of the day, although Fianna Fáil was also helped by the absence of a vote transfer arrangement between Fine Gael and Labour.

And four years later, in the general election of 1973, the very presence of such a Fine Gael/Labour electoral pact significantly limited the benefits of Boland's constituency redrawing. The strategy of three-seaters in rural areas had worked well for Fianna Fáil against a divided opposition but not when there were strong transfers between Fine Gael and Labour candidates – it meant each of the three parties was likely to end up with one seat, instead of Fianna Fáil taking two seats. Fianna Fáil did hold its seats in Dublin, where four-seaters predominated; however, against all the odds, Fianna Fáil managed to increase its first-preference vote, the party lost six seats and Fine Gael and Labour just about had the seats to form a new 'National Coalition'.

It should have served as a warning to governments that attempting to revise constituencies in their favour is a hazardous exercise. But it was a warning that was totally overlooked by the incoming government.

Act V

In 1974, the new Local Government Minister, Jim Tully of Labour, implemented what was effectively a reverse gerrymander – which to this day is still remembered as the 'Tullymander'. J.J. Lee later wrote that it 'was the sheer professionalism of his handiwork that earned his own arrangement the half-grudging description of Tullymander, threatening to consign the venerable Governor Gerry to semantic oblivion'. Tully effectively reversed what Boland had done a few years earlier. In Dublin, where Fianna Fáil was seen as weakest, he replaced the four seaters with 13 three-seaters, and went for four- and five-seaters in rural areas where Fianna Fáil was strongest. The goal was to limit Fianna Fáil to just one out of three seats in the capital's constituencies and just half the spoils in western constituencies where it was strongest. There were some minority voices in Fine Gael concerned about the move. Garret Fitzgerald objected at cabinet but the more widely-held view was summed up by one Fine Gael TD who later wrote, 'we all rejoiced in supporting the bill because we were at last getting even with Fianna Fáil, the real connoisseurs of manipulating constituency boundaries'. Most commentators also believed it was a masterstroke.

But they hadn't read the small print. There was a serious problem with Tully's plan. The Tullymander was fine if, as most people assumed, the coalition government received a roughly similar number of votes as it did in 1973. Analysis carried out by Fianna Fáil's Martin O'Donoghue in 1974 showed that if the new constituencies had been in place in the 1973 general election, it would have increased Fine Gael and Labour's majority from four to a much more handsome 14. However, O'Donoghue was one of the few to spot that Tully's proposal was vulnerable to any fall in the National Coalition's share of the vote in selected constituencies. O'Donoghue also later wrote that he thought Tully had erred in trying to maximise Labour's potential seat total.

But it was only with hindsight that the huge flaw in the Tullymander would really become obvious – sure, it would protect the government in the event of a minor swing against it, but any bigger swing to Fianna Fáil than that and the main opposition party could count on disproportionate gains. To be fair, nobody at the time believed a major swing against the government was likely at the time Tully was crunching the numbers but perhaps a worse case scenario should have been analysed because that is exactly what happened in the 1977 landslide. Fianna Fáil won 50.6 per cent of the vote and almost 57 per cent of the seats; its twenty-seat majority was by some margin the biggest in the history of the State.

With 50.6 per cent of the vote, Fianna Fáil would have comfortably won the election regardless of what Tully had done (and he could hardly be blamed for the dramatic collapse in the government parties' support). However, unquestionably the Tullymander ensured that Fianna Fáil's majority was much bigger. In Dublin, instead of winning one out of three seats, Fianna Fáil's thumping vote meant it took two out of three in many constituencies. And in four-seaters, it was also in the shake-up for three of the seats. Labour suffered particularly badly in the election, with two of their high profile ministers, Justin Keating and Conor Cruise O'Brien, losing their seats. Their departure meant there was no obvious successor to Brendan Corish who resigned as party leader immediately after the election, along with outgoing Taoiseach Liam Cosgrave.

Despite overseeing a massive increase in public housing during his ministry, the Tullymander disaster meant that Tully was not going to be a potential candidate. 'Tully suddenly found himself in near disgrace after his apparently foolproof constituency revision had so unsportingly backfired,' J.J. Lee wrote.

EPILOGUE

The Tullymander, however, did do the State some service. It was so blatant that it could never be allowed happen again. Jack Lynch, to his credit, delivered on a pre-election promise to establish an independent boundary review commission. The practice of the minister of the day dictating the make-up of the Dáil constituencies was, thankfully, at an end.

33

The Most Bitter General Election 1933

PROLOGUE

At the end of 1932 de Valera stunned the country, and his own party, by calling a general election for 24 January 1933 – less than a year after Fianna Fáil had wrestled power from Cumann na nGaedheal. That February 1932 victory, famous though it was, did not give Fianna Fáil a majority in the Dáil and de Valera's government was dependent on the support of the Labour Party. With Fianna Fáil taking a cautious approach to public finances, that support could not be taken for granted indefinitely. Labour was particularly restless about cabinet moves to cut the wages of certain public-sector workers and de Valera was clearly worried about his ability to govern effectively, given the Dáil arithmetic (Fianna Fáil held 72 seats out of 153 seats and were thus five short of a majority).

While it was certainly a gamble by de Valera, the timing for an election was particularly good – the new Fianna Fáil government had belied its minority position in the Dáil by rigorously setting about introducing its policies. The move to abolish the Oath of Allegiance, which had been delayed because the opposition controlled the Seanad, won popular support, as did the refusal to pay land annuities to the British government (although there was tension with farmers who, despite de Valera's desire that they continue the payment to the Irish government, simply stopped paying). The negative impact of the economic war with Britain, prompted by the refusal to pay the afore-mentioned annuities, was yet to manifest itself. The election came at a bad time for Cumann na nGaedheal and the rest of the opposition.

Cumann na nGaedheal was demoralised by its election defeat less than a year earlier and had provided very negative opposition. The National Centre Party, established from the remnants of the Farmers' Party and some independent TDs (including James Dillon, son of former Irish Parliamentary Party leader, John Dillon) had only just been formed. Labour, meanwhile, was in a position to nominate only 19 candidates. De Valera promised, during the short election campaign, that he would halve the land annuities if returned to office, but what really stood out about the election was the sheer bitterness of the campaign.

THE DRAMA

Tension had been building even before the general election. After Fianna Fáil was elected to government, it released IRA prisoners who had been jailed by the previous administration. Throughout 1932, bands of armed men disrupted Cumann na nGaedheal public meetings, declaring there should be 'no free speech for traitors'. In response the Army Comrades Association (ACA), founded in February 1932 and soon to be known as the Blueshirts, evolved into a rival quasi-miliatry group with a role to protect Cumann na nGaedheal members from harassment. The 1933 election saw running battles between the IRA and ACA (now led by Cumann na nGaedheal TD, TF O'Higgins, brother of the assassinated minister Kevin O'Higgins).

In his hugely informative book of *Irish Elections, 1918–1977*, Cornelius O'Leary describes the election campaign as the most bitter in the history of the state. 'The issue as posed by the government was a simple one of a small nation trying to free itself from unwanted ties with a large empire, and on that interpretation the opposition parties, whatever economic arguments they might advance, could be (and were) labelled anti-national. This line of argument brought the Treaty issue, in a somewhat new form, back sharply before the people's minds, and with it came the inevitable concomitant violence,' O'Leary wrote.

The Fianna Fáil government did use the Garda Síochána and even the army to keep public order during the campaign but, as O'Leary notes, Cumann na nGaedheal came to rely on the ACA rather than on the normal guardians of the law for their protection. However, their party was no match for the energy generated by the Fianna Fáil government and the electorate delivered a thumping victory for de Valera. Fianna Fáil's share of the vote had risen from 44.5 per cent eleven months earlier to 49.7 per cent and it had gained five seats, giving it 77 of the 153 seats.

It was the first time since independence that any party had won an overall majority. Michael Gallagher notes in his book, *Irish Elections 1922–44: Results and Analysis,* that Fianna Fáil made gains in all but six constituencies, with especially large advances in Dublin. Incredibly, it polled more than two-thirds of the votes in Kerry. Cumann na nGaedheal, in what would be its last election under that title, fell back further, with particularly heavy losses in Leinster outside Dublin. Labour, meanwhile, endured what remains its lowest ever share of the vote (5.7 per cent) and, incredible as it seems today, was left without a seat in Dublin. Other than Fianna Fáil, only the new National Centre Party took comfort from the election – it won 11 seats.

EPILOGUE

The high degree of polarisation had one clear benefit: a record turnout of 81.3 per cent of the electorate, which was extraordinary given the election was held in January. That turnout remains the highest ever achieved in the history of the State. As Gallagher notes, the polarisation was also reflected in the transfer pattern between the parties. The election demonstrated a party system consisting of two blocs – Fianna Fáil and Labour being one, and Cumann na nGaedheal and the National Centre Party being the other. Transfers within each bloc were extremely high, with very low numbers of transfers passing between the two blocs.

The new mandate received by de Valera strengthened his position in dealing with the private armies that had disrupted the election. He dismissed Eoin O'Duffy as Garda Commissioner the following month. Soon after O'Duffy assumed the leadership of the ACA. The organisation changed its name to the National Guard and began to take on some of the trappings of the Fascist parties in Europe at the time, most notably the wearing of a blue shirt (although as J.J. Lee points out in *Ireland 1912–1985*, the Blueshirts were not fascists but 'simply traditional conservatives decked out in fashionable but ideologically ill-fitting continental garb' whose goal was not revolution, but the restoration of 'the status quo ante'). Any threat the organisation did pose to democracy effectively ended in August of 1933 when de Valera faced down O'Duffy's plans for a march of the National Guard past the Dáil by banning both the march and the organisation itself.

The following month the Blueshirts, the Centre Party and Cumann na nGaedheal merged to form the United Ireland party, which became better known as Fine Gael, with O'Duffy as its leader. The violence between the IRA and the Blueshirts worsened in late 1933 as agricultural circumstances deteriorated. However, by the following year, it had become apparent that O'Duffy was a liability to the new Fine Gael party and he was forced to step down. The Blueshirt movement did not entirely die out until 1936 when O'Duffy left Ireland with some of his supporters to fight for Franco in the Spanish Civil War.

By that stage, de Valera had also declared the IRA illegal – many of its members fought on the Republican side in the Spanish Civil War. While both groups continued their opposition to each other in Spain, by the time of the next Irish general election in 1937 neither group would be a factor.

34

The Battle for Tang Church
1987

PROLOGUE

General election campaigns are not for the faint-hearted. It's a rough, tough business with few prisoners taken. But what makes Irish politics different from, say, across the water is that the most bitter and fierce rivalries are often not between candidates from opposing parties, as one would expect, but involve those sharing the same party ticket. It's back to our old friend PR-STV and the multi-seat constituencies. Particularly for the bigger parties, there are often two, three and even four candidates on their ticket in one constituency.

With all these candidates anxious to get to the Dáil and competing with each other for the attention of the voters, it's hardly surprising they often end up at each other's throats, metaphorically speaking of course. There is hardly a constituency in the country at general election time where there isn't tension between party running mates – usually over the division of the constituency for canvassing – and sometimes that spills over into virtual open warfare. Irish political history is packed with stories of rivalries between running mates: George Colley and Bertie Ahern in Dublin Central (see Chapter 47), Michael Ring and

Enda Kenny in Mayo, Síle de Valera and Tom Kitt in the days when de Valera ran in Dublin South, Mary O'Rourke and Donie Cassidy in Westmeath, Mary Fitzpatrick and Cyprian Brady in Dublin Central (see Chapter 8), Avril Doyle and Máiread McGuinness in the East constituency in the European elections, etc.

These examples represent just a fraction of those that have entered political folklore. And rest assured, for every one that made it into the public arena, there have been another ten kept under wraps. However, if any single incident sums up the type of tensions that exist between candidates from the same party, it is the one that took place outside the churchyard of a townland on the border of Longford and Westmeath – the so-called 'Battle for Tang Church'.

THE DRAMA

It was the general election of 1987. The outgoing Fine Gael and Labour government, after being in power during four grim years of recession, had no chance of being re-elected. The only question was whether Charlie Haughey could finally deliver an overall majority for Fianna Fáil or whether there would be a hung Dáil. Longford–Westmeath was one of the constituencies where Fianna Fáil was hoping to pick up an extra seat. In the general election of November 1982, despite Fianna Fáil having well over 50 per cent of the first-preference vote, the four seats had been divided equally between Fianna Fáil and Fine Gael.

The two Fianna Fáil TDs, Albert Reynolds and Mary O'Rourke, were both big names in the party and competition between the two at constituency level had always been pretty intense. However, the retirement of Fine Gael TD Gerry L'Estrange, allied to an inevitable drop in the Fine Gael vote from its high of 1982, meant there was a real opportunity for Fianna Fáil to take three out of four seats. Barrister Henry Abbott was the third name on the Fianna Fáil ticket, with his base of Mullingar giving the party a good geographical spread (O'Rourke was based in Athlone; Reynolds in Longford).

However, it would require tight vote management to deliver all three to the Dáil. Director of elections councillor Mickey Doherty warned party supporters: 'If we are going for three out of four seats, and we are, then the North Westmeath people will have to vote for the North Westmeath candidate [Abbot]; the South Westmeath people will have to vote for the South Westmeath candidate [O'Rourke]; and Longford people must vote entirely for the Longford candidate [Reynolds].' The worry for big name candidates such as Reynolds and O'Rourke in these situations is that when votes are being so tightly managed it increases the chances of a higher profile candidate – who would normally attract votes across the constituency – losing out.

Albert Reynolds was leaving nothing to chance. He cut down on TV and radio appearances for the national campaign and all seven members of his family were out on the campaign trail. Tensions between him and O'Rourke were running high and matters came to a head on a Sunday morning outside Tang Church. Tang, being in Westmeath, was assigned to O'Rourke. But as she and her team awaited the exit of Mass-goers for the traditional after-Mass meeting, they were stunned to observe Reynolds and his activists also arriving.

In his biography of Albert Reynolds, *The Longford Leader*, Tim Ryan described how one of O'Rourke's team was overheard shouting: 'Holy f**k, look who has arrived.'

Ryan wrote that 'having parked their cars out of sight of the church, there was Reynolds leading his gang of activists down the middle of the road towards the church. To say there was a look of panic on O'Rourke's face is an understatement.'

Not surprisingly, one of O'Rourke's team challenged Reynolds, asking: 'What the f**k are you doing here? This is Westmeath and O'Rourke territory, and you have no f**king business here.' However, the future Taoiseach replied that he was entitled to be there as people from nearby Ballymahon in County Longford – Reynolds' territory – went to Mass in Tang.

Almost two decades later, speaking in the Seanad, O'Rourke referred to the incident at Tang, telling the House: 'As one approaches the townland there is a sign which states 'Welcome to County Westmeath', but the people of Ballymahon go to Mass in Tang. They have two masses in Tang said by a priest who believes in short masses . . . I arrived at the church with my truck, my guys and my microphone. Then Albert arrived with his truck, his guys and his microphone, and it became a question of what would happen. We knew the priest was nearing completion in the church because we had a scout going inside to keep us informed. We did not know what would happen or whether we were going to drown out one another. However, a very nice councillor from Longford said "Get up on the one truck the two of ye. Aren't ye both Fianna Fáil?" We did, and we said our piece.'

Ryan, though, wrote that in retaliation for Reynolds' incursion into O'Rourke's territory, one of O'Rourke's entourage was dispatched to Ballymahon, with his vegetable truck adorned with her posters, to drive up and down the street while Reynolds addressed an after-Mass meeting. Not surprisingly Reynolds took 'a dim view' of the action, Ryan wrote. But it was clearly a case of 'you scratch my patch, I'll scratch yours'.

34 – The Battle for Tang Church

EPILOGUE

Whatever about Reynolds and O'Rourke both winning the 'Battle for Tang Church', they certainly both won the war. In the general election, with Fine Gael's vote collapsing, Fianna Fáil won three out of the four seats in the constituency – Reynolds topped the poll, followed by Abbot and then O'Rourke. As is so often the case, the tension between the candidates worked well for Fianna Fáil, helping to maximise its votes.

Fianna Fáil returned to government, albeit yet again without an overall majority, and both O'Rourke and Reynolds were in the new cabinet. However, the tension between the two did not disappear in the aftermath of Tang. Five years later Reynolds defeated O'Rourke in a leadership contest to become leader of Fianna Fáil and Taoiseach. He then proceeded to drop O'Rourke, among others, from his new cabinet.

It was probably just as well that by then the two politicians were in different constituencies, with Westmeath becoming a stand-alone three-seater after 1989. There was also a nice little historical irony about the incident at Tang church. The aforementioned town of Ballymahon was so-called because it was the site of a victory by Brian Boru's older brother, Mahon, who defeated – you've guessed it – the O'Rourkes, laying claim to land in the area. A thousand years on and it seems only the form of battle has changed.

35

The Twenty-Five County Dáil
2007

PROLOGUE

The beauty of a liberal democracy in a republic is that, theoretically, any man or woman can rise to be a member of parliament, or even prime minister/head of state, on merit alone, regardless of their circumstances, background, wealth, etc. Of course, it doesn't really work out like that. As we know from Irish politics, your background certainly helps. Coming from a political family (see Chapter 40) or being a high-profile GAA figure is a definite advantage if you want to get ahead in politics.

And while it is certainly not necessary to be born with a silver spoon in your mouth to succeed in Irish politics, 'rags to riches' stories are sadly few enough. It has also emerged that where you come from in the country can have a serious impact on your chances of getting into the Dáil, and subsequently of being promoted.

THE DRAMA

The Seanad elections of July 2007 threw up an unwanted first in

Irish politics. With long-time Senator Pascal Mooney surprisingly losing his seat and Enda McGloin falling short, Leitrim was shaping up to become the first county that failed to have a single member of the Oireachtas. There was some slight remedying of the situation when Taoiseach Bertie Ahern surprisingly named former Leitrim Fianna Fáil TD John Ellis as one of his nominations to the Seanad. But it was small consolation for the people of Leitrim, given what happened in the general election earlier in the summer.

Leitrim was divided, for the first time, between two constituencies (Sligo–North Leitrim and Roscommon–South Leitrim) and the result saw all six deputies coming from either Sligo or Roscommon. Leitrim's best hope of a seat was Ellis, who was first elected to the Dáil in 1981 and had been returned at every subsequent election bar one since then. However, despite polling almost 8,000 votes in Roscommon–South Leitrim he didn't succeed.

The result of the general election confirmed the worst fears of the 'Save Leitrim Campaign', who had argued against the Boundary Commission's decision to split the country's least populated county in two for electoral purposes. They warned that such a decision would leave the county without a TD and were proved correct. 'This will impact on every facet of people's lives from schools to health to getting funding for a sports club. As it stands, people living in south Leitrim have to travel 50 miles to their nearest government TD. Is this accessibility to government?' asked a spokesman for the 'Save Leitrim Campaign'.

The campaign is hoping that the county will be unified by the latest boundary commission's report at the end of 2007. Leitrim is also the only county never to have had a minister at the cabinet table. And it only ever had a junior minister for a brief period in the 1970s. 'Being born and living in County Leitrim is a guaranteed way of becoming a failed Dáil candidate as the recent general election results demonstrate,' was the verdict of one of the submissions from Leitrim to the new boundary commission. It's hard to disagree.

EPILOGUE

Whereas the entire county of Leitrim was left without representation by the Dáil and Seanad elections of 2007, the tiny village of Ahascragh in Galway, in contrast, enjoyed an embarrassment of riches in the Oireachtas – six serving members of the two houses were born there or in its surrounding townlands. The Minister for Health, Mary Harney, hails from the village as do the three Kitt siblings: chief whip Tom, junior minister Michael and sister Áine Brady, a newly-elected TD. Labour leader Eamon Gilmore is also from the area, while the sextet is completed by surprise Seanad victor Ronan Mullen. Of the six, however, only Michael Kitt actually represents Ahascragh in the Oireachtas.

Leitrim's political famine is also put into context by comparison with leafy Dublin South-East. Since the foundation of the state, what is arguably the country's wealthiest constituency has provided two Taoisigh, three Tánaiste, two Ministers for Finance, six party leaders and three Presidents. How's that for influence?

36

Who Feared to Stand in '38
1938

PROLOGUE

In general elections nowadays every constituency is fiercely fought. As well as several candidates from the two big parties and a selection from Labour, Sinn Féin, the PDs, the Greens and the Socialist Party, there is likely to be a range of independents hoping, and sometimes succeeding against the odds, to pull off a surprise and take a seat. However, elections have not always been so strongly contested.

In Chapter 30 there is an analysis of the general election of 1921, when every single constituency in the 26 counties was uncontested (still a record in a Western democracy). But that was an unusual situation as the country was at war. More surprising are the times, post independence, when constituencies remained uncontested – most notably in the general election of 1938. There had been a general election less than a year earlier, which saw de Valera and Fianna Fáil returned but without an absolute overall majority. After what was perceived as his triumph in negotiating an end to the Economic War with Britain, de Valera called a snap election in order to secure that majority.

THE DRAMA

De Valera's landslide win is dealt with elsewhere (see Chapter 38), but what concerns us here is that two three-seat constituencies – South Kerry and Donegal West – had no contests, while concerted but unsuccessful efforts were also made to avoid contests in Leitrim, Wicklow and Wexford. So, before even a vote was counted in the general election of June 1938, the six TDs from South Kerry and Donegal were, along with the Ceann Comhairle of the previous Dáil, automatically returned to the tenth Dáil.

On polling day, de Valera already knew that he had five of the 70 seats he needed for an overall majority in the bag. Fine Gael held the other two. Viewed from a 70-year distance, it is perhaps difficult to understand the reasoning behind the lack of a contest in those constituencies. But there was presumably a logic behind the decisions of those involved (or not involved). Fianna Fáil were obviously happy with the *status quo* as it had two out of the three seats in both South Kerry and Donegal West and was never going to win a third seat in either. The two Fianna Fáil incumbents in each case were, for obvious reasons, not keen to take on a running mate and any potential challengers in the party probably felt the TDs *in situ* couldn't be beaten.

As Professor Michael Gallagher of Trinity College points out, it was common, when one election closely followed another, for the number of independents and candidates from minor parties to decline. An independent candidate had stood in South Kerry in 1937, but he may have seen little point in running again so soon after failing to come close to winning a seat.

Perhaps the only surprise was Fine Gael's failure to run second candidates in the two constituencies, as it had done eleven months earlier. South Kerry is less puzzling as Fine Gael had no real prospect of a second seat there, but in Donegal West a small swing would have given it a second seat (hindsight showed that with the massive increase in Fianna Fáil's vote, this wouldn't have happened).

Again, one can only presume the second Fine Gael candidate from 1937 saw little chance of unseating the incumbent Fine Gael TD who was obviously happy for him not to run, given that his seat would probably have been the most vulnerable. In their book, *Days of Blue Loyalty*, Gallagher and his fellow Trinity professor Michael Marsh refer to the lack of any coherent Fine Gael organisation during that era. Local organisations, such as they were, don't seem to have been under the control of national headquarters. Six years later the party didn't even contest by-elections because it couldn't find credible candidates (see Chapter 18), so no doubt the poor state of Fine Gael's organisation was a factor in the no-contests in South Kerry and Donegal West.

Elsewhere Fine Gael did get its act together to nominate a second candidate in Leitrim – just about. It had looked like the two Fianna Fáil and one Fine Gael TDs would be returned unopposed, but a second Fine Gael candidate was nominated just five minutes before the deadline. Presumably the candidature was left so late to discourage any other potential challengers from entering the fray. Either way, it didn't matter much – the three incumbents were comfortably returned.

The efforts to avoid contests in Wicklow and Wexford seemed to be centred around the celebrations for the 140th anniversary of the 1798 rebellion. In Wexford, the '98 Commemoration Association requested that the constituency be uncontested. This seems like a surprising stance; surely the best way to commemorate the rising was with a free and competitive election?

In its editorial in the run-up to the election, the *Wicklow People* lamented the holding of another election so soon after the last, stating that it interfered with the business and trade of the county. It also outlined the thinking behind the calls for agreed candidates in Wicklow and Wexford. 'Such an action would have the effect of a non-resurrection of party strife,' the paper said.

While it agreed that 'the idea has much to recommend it and is made with the worthiest of motives,' the *People* ultimately came down against the concept. 'There would be many found to be dissatisfied were they deprived of the opportunity that has presented itself of expressing by their votes their opinions of recent actions of the government of Éire. In doing that, they will not be estranging any friendships or causing any political feuds, only discharging the task placed on them as electors,' the newspaper concluded. Obviously the memories of the bitter elections of 1932 and especially 1933 remained potent. A later edition of the *Wicklow People* also warned that a 'no-contest' might provoke apathy among electors.

Despite this inarguable logic, the paper reported there had been efforts to get one of the four candidates in three-seat Wicklow to withdraw – presumably Patrick Cogan who was an independent/Farmers' Party candidate (and later a member of both Clann na Talmhan and Fianna Fáil). However, in a seminal lesson to those who sought to avoid the contest, Cogan ended up taking a seat by 130 votes from Fine Gael TD 'The O'Mahony'.

In Wexford, there was also a contest with the five TDs – two Fianna Fáil, two Fine Gael, one Labour – being challenged, as in the election eleven months earlier, by one extra candidate from both Fianna Fáil and Fine Gael. The result was virtually identical however, with the five TDs being returned in the same order.

EPILOGUE

Competition came slowly to Kerry South and Donegal West after 1938. At the next election there was a contest in Kerry South with two independents and one Labour candidate. But it would be 1948 before there would be a change in the 2:1 Fianna Fáil / Fine Gael carve-up. Ironically, it was former Fianna Fáil TD John Flynn, one of the three returned unopposed in 1938, who won the seat as an independent in 1948 in a highly competitive contest with eight candidates, including two from Clann na Phoblachta.

Matters moved even more slowly in Donegal West. There was a contest in 1943 because two Labour candidates and one independent challenged the two Fianna Fáil TDs and one Fine Gael TD, but they fell short. And when de Valera called another snap general election the following year, the contestants fell away, leaving another uncontested election in Donegal West. The three TDs – Brian Brady (FF), Cormac Breslin (FF) and Michael McFadden (FG) – who were returned unopposed in 1944 had also been the three returned without a contest in 1938.

However, that was the last time that there was an uncontested election in the State.

37

Spring's Winter of Content
1982

PROLOGUE

For any leader of a political party, a general election is a particularly stressful time. It's the time for the leader to deliver. A good performance – elevating the party to, or retaining it in, government – and the leader is a hero. A bad performance that sees the party dropping seats and returning to, or staying on, the opposition benches, and he or she could be on the way out. Now imagine being just 32 years old, having just 18 months under your belt in the Dáil (a good deal of which was spent in hospital after a horrific car crash), becoming a divided and declining party's fourth leader in just five years and then, within days of this promotion to leader, having to face into a general election that threatened to be one of the most traumatic in its history.

Far-fetched? Unthinkable? Not at all – that's exactly the scenario that Dick Spring faced when he was propelled from nowhere into the leadership of the Labour Party on 1 November 1982. Three days after becoming leader of the Labour Party and just two hours after he delivered his first major speech in the Dáil on a motion of no-confidence in Charlie Haughey's crisis-ridden 'GUBU' government, the Dáil had been dissolved and Spring was facing into a general-election campaign. And facing into it with a party – as his close advisor Fergus Finlay later wrote – that was 'demoralised, terribly split, and above all, a virtual stranger to its leader'. Brian Boru himself might have crumbled under half that pressure.

THE DRAMA

Before November 1982, Dick Spring was probably still best known as a rugby player who had been capped several times at fullback for Ireland. His father Dan had been a TD for Kerry North for four decades, with Dick, a trained barrister, taking over the seat in the election of 1981 (thereby instantly becoming a junior minister in the short-lived Fine Gael/Labour government that lost power over the 'VAT on children's shoes' budget).

However, in those weeks leading up to Christmas 1982, Spring would go from being just another politician to being arguably the second most powerful man in national politics. Not for the first time, Labour was tearing itself apart on the issue of coalition government and had spent the previous two years engaging in what Finlay described as 'one of its interminable internal battles about ideological purity'.

Spring's predecessor as Labour Party leader, Michael O'Leary, had sought to obtain coalition endorsement at the party's annual conference in Galway on 23 October. However, this was defeated with the party opting instead for a post-election delegate conference on the issue. O'Leary responded five days later by resigning both his leadership and membership of the party. Less than a week later, it was announced that O'Leary wished to join Fine Gael and that its leader Garret FitzGerald would be recommending this to his party. The blow to Labour could hardly have been greater and, to make matters worse, it was now clear that a general election was inevitable as Charlie Haughey's minority 'GUBU' government had been defeated in a confidence motion. It wasn't just O'Leary's defection the new young leader of the Labour Party had to worry about. Opinion polls showed Labour's bitter rival, the Workers' Party, was enjoying increased support, while Labour's support was static. The Workers' Party's decision to withdraw its support in the Dáil for Haughey's government was believed to be influenced by this strength in the opinon polls, plus the disarray in the Labour camp. The election of a novice to the Labour leadership was an added bonus. Little wonder that every political commentator was predicting Labour's decimation in the general election.

However, Spring was to surprise everybody. As Bruce Arnold wrote in *What Kind of Country?*, Spring 'took to leadership with a coolness and strength of purpose that was quite astonishing'. He cobbled together an election manifesto by early the following week, which was launched at a press conference where the party managed to present an image of solid party unity – something it had not always managed in the past, to put it mildly. Spring also showed that he would be his own man. Rather than instructing supporters to transfer votes to Fine Gael, he said they should transfer votes to those candidates most in line with Labour's policies and objectives. The slight shift in emphasis went down well with the party faithful. Despite this, Spring was committed to removing Fianna Fáil and, particularly, Charlie Haughey from power.

One week into his leadership and Labour's fortunes were already looking better. 'He looks like a leader,' wrote John Healy approvingly in *The Irish Times*. 'It was as if the new Labour leader had pulled his party together to such an extent that it entered upon the election campaign with its own internal crises firmly behind it,' wrote Bruce Arnold later. The election turned out to be a remarkable triumph (albeit a relative one) against the odds for Dick Spring and Labour. The party's vote held firm, even going up slightly, and it added a seat, ending up with 16 deputies (in comparison, the Workers' Party lost a seat and ended up with just two TDs). With Fine Gael winning its highest ever seat total of 70, it and Labour had a clear majority in the new Dáil.

But it was a case of 'out of the frying pan into the fire' for Spring. Having survived potential meltdown in the general election, he then had to agree a deal on coalition with the highly experienced Garret FitzGerald that he could sell to his party. Fergus Finlay later wrote in his book, *Snakes and Ladders*, that it was 'the toughest, and loneliest, negotiations he [Spring] ever conducted'. Fine Gael sought to take every advantage possible of Spring's inexperience. 'A politician with no background or training in economic policy was expected to negotiate with Garret FitzGerald and Alan Dukes about how the currency could be stabilised, and about how the spiralling public expenditure could be managed,' Finlay wrote.

The negotiations took place in a convent in Donnybrook, on the southside of Dublin, mainly to keep the media at bay. However, as Finlay pointed out, 'if it also helped ensure the inexperienced Labour leader was isolated from whatever back-up and support he could count on, so much the better'. Fine Gael introduced Peter Sutherland to the negotiations on their side, perhaps for his legal/constitutional expertise, or perhaps, as Finlay observed, because 'he was a much more senior figure at the bar than Dick and this would automatically put Dick at a disadvantage'.

The final proof that Spring was being played came when

37 – Spring's Winter of Content

FitzGerald told him he was taking three days off from the negotiations to attend a European Christian Democratic conference in Paris. It was then Spring showed a steely side that would emerge on a number of occasions over the next 15 years. He regarded it as unthinkable that a party leader would choose to leave the negotiations to underlings and made it clear that if FitzGerald didn't forget Paris, the negotiations were over. Garret never did go to that conference. Helped by a few close friends, advisors and a couple of senior Labour TDs, a coalition deal was forged. Spring managed to get it through a special delegate conference the following weekend. Two days later the new Fine Gael/Labour government was formed.

In what was probably the most rapid rise since the early days of the State, Spring became Tánaiste and Minister for Environment in the new government – some achievement for a man in national politics for just 18 months.

EPILOGUE

Despite that, things didn't get become any easier for Spring over the next few years. It was probably the worst time since the 1950s to be in power. The government was bogged down in debt and had literally no money to spend; unemployment was rising sharply and the coalition seemed to lurch from one crisis to the next. Four years later, Spring hung onto his seat by the narrowest of margins – just four extra votes enabled him to return to the Dáil at the expense of Tom McEllistrum. That general election saw Fianna Fáil returned to office, dumping Spring and Labour to the back benches.

But the lessons learned since November 1982 would be put to

good use. A decade on from his baptism of fire, Spring and Labour would fight another general election. This time the party was completely united; Spring had faced down the dissidents on the left, and the Labour leader, far from being an inexperienced novice, had been the most impressive political performer of the previous three years. As part of what became known as the 'Spring tide', his party won 19 per cent of the vote and 33 seats – the best performance in its history.

There would be more coalition negotiations to conduct, but this time Spring was in the position of strength. Fianna Fáil and Fine Gael needed Labour, not the other way around. This time Spring was calling the shots.

38

How Dev Bit the Bullet
1923

PROLOGUE

It was August 1923 and an election campaign was in full swing. But this was no ordinary election. The horrendously bitter Civil War had just ended and many on the defeated Republican side were still on the run. Included in this number was Éamon de Valera, the former President of the Dáil who had resigned 18 months earlier over the Treaty. Although a minor figure on the military side of the Civil War, he remained the political head of the anti-Treaty side.

When the election was called, a convention of Sinn Féin candidates sent a message from Ennis town hall asking de Valera to once again stand in the constituency as their unanimous first choice. Despite being on the run, de Valera had vowed that if the people of Clare selected him as their candidate 'nothing but a bullet will stop me' being with them. There was considerable danger for him in appearing in the open. It was said that some members of the Free State CID were being 'roused' to assassinate de Valera by stories that he had personally planned the death of Michael Collins. However, in the biography, *Eamon de Valera* by Lord Longford and Thomas P O'Neill, it is noted that de Valera felt that by coming out of hiding he would 'definitely transfer the struggle from the military to the political field'.

THE DRAMA

On 12 August, de Valera, after making his will, set out for Clare, guided by IRA officer Sean Hyde. They had put out a rumour that de Valera would travel to Clare by sea, but instead they kept mainly to the north of the Dublin–Limerick road, arriving in Knockanira, five miles south-west of Ennis. A last-minute decision not to move to a house beside the square in Ennis proved fortuitous as it was raided by the Free State army that night.

De Valera wanted to be on the platform if arrested, to prove his claim that the election was not free. Presumably to avert a propaganda coup for the Republican side, the Free State troops were under orders to arrest de Valera before he appeared in public. The night before making his appearance, de Valera shaved off the beard and moustache he had grown – 'he was not going to appear in disguise among the people in Clare,' Longford and O'Neill wrote.

On the afternoon of 15 August – the Feast of Our Lady – de Valera was driven in an open-top car to the square in Ennis and successfully mounted the platform without being recognised. The intense cheering told the watching Free State troops they had failed to stop him doing so. Their commander ordered an officer to take a party of soldiers and arrest de Valera on the platform. De Valera had just started speaking when firing broke out and chaos descended on the square as a Free State armoured-car came through the crowd. According to Longford and O'Neill's account, de Valera felt a 'sharp pain in his left leg . . . He thought his shinbone had been broken by a bullet. Those on the platform behind him pulled him backwards among them. Gradually the pain eased and life returned to his numbed leg. He rose amid cheering and was able to make his way down the steps to the soldiers and to walk to the barracks with the officers who arrested him.' Mission accomplished.

EPILOGUE

When de Valera examined his leg later that day, he found a small blob of blood beside his shin bone. Forty years later, by which point de Valera was president, an X-ray revealed a piece of bullet – most probably from a ricochet – lodged in the muscle of his leg. Longford and O'Neill wrote that what interested de Valera most of all was that he could find no tear in the leg of his trousers (although one hopes he didn't still have them four decades on).

In the election later that month, de Valera topped the poll with a huge 17,762 votes: 45% of the votes cast and more than twice the number received by government minister Eoin MacNeill. Indeed, de Valera got so many votes that his transfers were sufficient to elect another Republican candidate, Brian O'Higgins, who had maanaged to win just 114 first-preference votes (see Chapter 27).

The following July, de Valera was released from Arbour Hill prison. Within two years he had established Fianna Fáil, within three years he had entered Dáil Éireann and within eight years he was head of a Fianna Fáil government. He would go on to spend a total of two decades as President of the Executive Council/ Taoiseach, and another 14 years as President of Ireland. But the road to the top started with that long journey to Ennis town square. The bullet fragment in the leg had been well worth it.

Trajectory of bullet

39

Fianna Fáil's Record Breaker
1938

PROLOGUE

There is no arguing with Fianna Fáil's dominance of Irish politics over the past 80 years. Since it first got into government in 1932, it has been in power for almost three out of every four years. The party's record in general elections since 1932 reads as follows: played 24, won 19 (albeit with some scrappy results), lost just 5.

In six of those general elections, the party has won an overall majority – an extremely difficult feat given the PR-STV electoral system – and, on another two occasions, it won exactly half the seats on offer. In two of those six overall majorities, Fianna Fáil managed to win an absolute majority of the votes cast, an extremely rare achievement under any electoral system anywhere.

Anybody with even half an interest in politics can identify one of those instances; the infamous general election of 1977 when Fianna Fáil stunned the political commentators (who had expected the Fine Gael/Labour coalition to be returned) by winning 50.6 per cent of the vote. The huge support for Fianna Fáil in that election didn't merely neuter the painstaking efforts by the coalition government to redraw Dáil constituencies to their own advantage (see Chapter 32), it actually ensured this attempt backfired on the government and worked instead to Fianna Fáil's advantage. Jack Lynch and Fianna Fáil won almost 60 per cent of the seats in the Dáil – a massive 20-seat majority. However, that 1977 landslide, while Fianna Fáil's most famous victory, was not actually the party's best-ever electoral performance. That honour goes to the Éamon de Valera-inspired performance in the 1938 general election.

THE DRAMA

The 1938 Fianna Fáil victory can be put down to de Valera's extraordinary ability to get the timing of elections just right. A year earlier, in the election of July 1937, Fianna Fáil had been re-elected to government. The party was just shy of an overall majority as it had half the Dáil seats. However, de Valera still had a seriously good card to play. Throughout 1937 and the early months of 1938, he had been negotiating with Britain in an effort to bring an end to the Economic War between the two countries.

A deal was reached in April 1938, involving an end to tariffs on Irish goods; an end to preferential treatment for British goods in Ireland; a lump sum of £10m in settlement of the land annuities dispute; and, crucially, given that World War II was only a year away, the handover to the Irish government of the three ports (Berehaven, Cobh and Lough Swilly that Britain had retained jurisdiction over as part of the Treaty).

While there was compromise involved on both sides, the securing of the ports made it a clear political triumph for de Valera. And with little delay, he called an election for 17 June, just eleven months after the last general election. As in 1933 when he called a snap election, it proved to be a masterful decision. Fianna Fáil won a staggering 51.9 per cent of the vote and 76 of the 138 seats – a 14-seat majority. The party gained votes in all but two constituencies and was the strongest in all but three. It won more than 60 per cent of the vote in five constituencies. The top nine vote-winners were all from Fianna Fáil. Its dominance was total and all encompassing.

It helped, of course, that Fine Gael was largely going through the motions for that election. It put forward just 76 candidates (down from 95 a year earlier); virtually all of them would have to win if the party was to be in a position to form a single-party government. Nor did it help that the party opposed the agreement reached between de Valera and the British, a stance that seemed to contradict everything Fine Gael and its predecessor, Cumann na nGaedheal, had stood for since the Treaty.

EPILOGUE

While Fine Gael was in a downward spiral – from which it would not emerge for another decade - de Valera was at the height of his powers (incredibly it was another 21 years before he finally abdicated to make way for Seán Lemass). Fianna Fáil had changed, irrevocably. 'From being a hungry fighter on the outside, it had moved to capture the middle ground, and to become increasingly an umbrella party of the centre,' wrote J.J. Lee in *Ireland 1912–85*. Even *The Irish Times* had come on board. 'We are glad that he [de Valera] has been returned to power,' it wrote when the election result came in.

Lee summed it up when he said that 'de Valera had established himself as the guarantor of social and political stability. A quiet election allowed voters to reflect on the calm haven into which the Taoiseach, whom many had distrusted as an erratic helmsman intent on churning up the waters, now seemed to have safely steered the ship of state.' Unfortunately, the ship was to run into some choppy seas during the 1940s and 1950s before a radical rethink on economic and industrial policy steered it to calmer waters.

Regardless of the conditions, the hugely convincing election result of 1938 was proof positive that Fianna Fáil was now the natural party of government – a position it has hung on to with admirable (or, for its detractors, frustrating) tenacity ever since.

40

Family Favourites
1959

PROLOGUE

Nepotism is not unique to Irish politics. Think about it: two of the last three leaders of the greatest power in the world have come from the same family. The much used British expression 'Bob's your uncle' is believed to have come from the 3rd Marquess of Salisbury – Christian name Robert – promoting his nephew, Arthur Balfour, to the sought-after post of chief secretary for Ireland.

However, compared to other Western liberal democracies, nepotism does seem to be particularly ingrained in the Irish political system. In Britain, if an MP dies in office you rarely see the late politician's wife, husband, son or daughter contesting the by-election – yet it is a regular occurrence in Ireland. Over 30 of the TDs in the current Dáil were preceded by a family member; the same goes for a third of the current cabinet. Two families account for six current TDs, while there are a number of politicians around today whose fathers and grandfathers have also served in the Dáil. Of the eleven men who have been Taoiseach (or President of the Executive Council in the case of William T Cosgrave), only two – Jack Lynch and Albert Reynolds – have

not had either a father, a son, a grandson or a brother who was also elected to the Dáil. The reasons for this are varied: the essentially local and personal nature of Irish life and politics, the benefit of a high-profile name, and the PR-STV electoral system being but three reasons.

THE DRAMA

A story told by James Dillon, leader of Fine Gael from 1959 to 1965, about his election to the Dáil in 1932, probably best sums up why, when searching for a new candidate, political parties like to keep it in the family. Dillon's father, John, was the last leader of the Irish Parliamentary Party. Sixteen years after his father's party was wiped out by Sinn Féin, James was seeking election as an independent nationalist candidate in Donegal. Dillon freely admitted afterwards that the main factor in his election was his father's name.

As recounted in Maurice Manning's biography of the Fine Gael leader, Dillon recalled a visit to a polling station in Gweedore. 'As I was leaving I met an old man and an old woman, who had just come out from voting, and I asked them quite jocularly, "Who did ye vote for?" The old man stopped and looked at me (he hadn't the faintest idea who I was). "Who would I vote for," he said, "but John Dillon's son? Herself and meself walked seven miles down from the mountain to vote for John Dillon's son, and we'll walk seven miles back, and it's not much thanks for all he did for us.'

EPILOGUE

In his biography of Dillon – who it should be noted was a fine politician and one of the greatest orators in the history of Dáil Éireann – Maurice Manning notes that his father's legacy had got Dillon into the Dáil and would help keep him there, but not indefinitely. The same goes for all those politicians since then (and there have been dozens) who have been elected primarily because of their family name. If they do not perform, their name will not keep them in the Dáil indefinitely. But the majority of them probably wouldn't be there in the first place if one of their relatives hadn't blazed a trail first.

If a famous surname can convince an elderly couple to walk 14 miles up and down a mountain to vote for this name, it clearly gives any family member an advantage over a candidate without a family background in politics. As the saying goes, as gaeilge, *Tús maith leath na hoibre.*

41

The Soldiers Fulfill Their Destiny
1932

PROLOGUE

There have been 30 general elections in the nine decades of Dáil Éireann but the election of 1932 stands out as the most dramatic of them all. Cumann na nGaedheal had been in power for the previous decade but, just six years after being formed, Fianna Fáil – led by the charismatic 1916 leader Éamon de Valera – was ready for government. The election had everything – excitement, tension, violence and concerns about a military coup. But when all the votes were counted, the fledgling Irish democracy emerged secure at a time when, across Europe, totalitarian regimes were taking power. It was the seventh election to the Dáil and its success ensured that the next 23 elections would be free and fair.

THE DRAMA

Act I

It was a contest between two titans, although the title holder was clearly past its best. Cumann na nGaedheal had without question performed extremely well in building up the new State, but image-wise the party had a problem. It was seen as conservative, increasingly remote from the general public (typified by their wearing of formal morning suits and top hats), overly parsimonious and austere, in favour of anti-working class policies and hung up on defending the Treaty of a decade earlier. It was vulnerable to the hungry and populist new challenger and it didn't help that its policy platform was wholly lacking in innovation, concentrating on law and order, religion and the 'red scare'; the chaos caused by a Fianna Fáil victory would bring irreligion and communism to the Republic, the party argued. In contrast, while not averse to playing the Catholic card, Fianna Fáil had an exciting programme of economic and social reform – including promises of a housing programme and the abolition of land annuities – that appealed to both urban and rural voters. The abolition of the Oath of Allegiance, which the government party had curiously clung to, was also central to its election manifesto. 'The electorate,' as J.J. Lee put it in *Ireland 1912–1985*, 'was therefore offered a clear choice between a party campaigning in defence of the status quo, and a party proposing sweeping constitutional, economic and social changes.'

When it came to organisation and image, Fianna Fáil were also far ahead of the rather dull Cumann na nGaedheal campaign. In *People, Politics and Power – From O'Connell to Ahern*, Stephen Collins describes how before addressing a Fianna Fáil public meeting, de Valera – dressed in a long black cape – would mount a white horse and proceed into the town, 'flanked by a band of horsemen with blazing sods of turf held aloft on pitchforks'. As Collins notes, the 'electrifying effect of this entrance to a drab Irish provincial town on a dark winter evening can only be imagined.' In contrast, William T Cosgrave's tour of the country was more sedate, involving a fair amount of dining with local bishops.

Cumann na nGaedheal's campaign was hugely negative, even if

some of its posters were highly entertaining. 'The Shadow of a Gunman – Keep it from your Door', said one. 'We want no Reds, keep their colour off your Flag' said another, while one of the party's newspaper adverts read: 'The gunmen are voting Fianna Fáil, the communists are voting Fianna Fáil'. An ad on the eve of polling day said that Fianna Fáil would give a free hand to the 'communists and terrorists'.

The most famous government poster of all went as follows: 'Devvy's Circus, absolutely the greatest roadshow in Ireland today – Señor de Valera, world-famous illusionist, oath-swallower and escapologist. See his renowned act: escaping from the straitjacket of the republic. Frank F. Aiken, fearsome fire-eater. Shaunty O'Kelly, the man in dress clothes. Monsieur Lemass, famous tightrope performer: see him cross from the Treaty to the Republic every night. Performing frogs, champion croakers, marvellous trained sheep.'

The campaign on the ground was electrifying, although not always for the right reasons. To his immense credit, de Valera fought the campaign with dignity, conscious of the impact his election would have on his enemies. But there was IRA muscle behind the Fianna Fáil campaign. In *The Cosgrave Legacy*, Stephen Collins describes how Cumann na nGaedheal speakers found it difficult to get a hearing on platforms. The shout would go up: 'Who started the Civil War?' or 'Who ordered the execution of Rory O'Connor?' The most common Cumann na nGaedheal response was: 'And how many banks did you rob?' The traditional eve of election rallies in Dublin were marked by fighting, with the *Irish Independent* reporting that gardaí had difficulty quelling the riot. 'There were cheers and counter cheers. Scuffles took place among the crowds. Free fights developed and batons were drawn,' the newspaper reported.

41 – The Soldiers Fulfill Their Destiny

Act II

The result of the election was a shattering blow for Cumann na nGaedheal. The people that the party had defeated in the Civil War a decade earlier had come back to beat them soundly at the ballot box. Fianna Fáil increased its vote from 35.2 per cent to 44.5 per cent, gaining 15 seats to 72 (five short of a majority). Cumann na nGaedheal dropped from 38.7 per cent to 35.3 per cent of the vote, losing five seats to 57. While it had the support of the Farmers' Party and independents, Labour had been more inclined towards Fianna Fáil during the campaign – as reflected in its transfers – and would vote for de Valera as Taoiseach. The sharp increase in turnout, from 69 per cent of the electorate five years earlier to 77 per cent in 1932, was a reflection of the excitement and interest generated by the campaign. Although that figure would be surpassed a year later (see Chapter 33).

Act III

However, the real drama centred on the Dáil on 9 March 1932, the day that de Valera was due to be elected Taoiseach. There were widespread fears that his election would be pre-empted by a coup. De Valera was accompanied to the Dáil by his son Vivion, who had a revolver in his pocket. Other senior Fianna Fáil TDs were armed as they entered the Dáil chamber and there were rumours that heavier weaponry was on hand in case of a coup. In *The Cosgrave Legacy*, Stephen Collins details how James Dillon, then an independent TD, claimed years later that he had seen a senior Fianna Fáil politician assembling a machine gun in a telephone booth at the back of the chamber.

However, while the enormous tension was understandable given the stakes and the Civil War enmity, with the benefit of hindsight it is clear that the chances of a coup happening were fairly remote.

Although there may have been one or two on the Cumann na nGaedheal side that were not overly committed to democracy, this did not include key figures such as Cosgrave and Richard Mulcahy. Their ten years of government were based on the principle of majority rights and, as men of honour, they weren't going to change that simply because they no longer had that majority. They were absolutely determined that the people's will would be exercised and there would be a smooth transition of power. Assurances from de Valera that there would be no victimisation of Treaty supporters also helped calm nerves. The one man who seemed to be cool as a cucumber during that day was Cosgrave. Maurice Manning's biography of James Dillon quotes Dillon saying that 'before the vote, far from being engaged in any frantic plotting, Cosgrave was upstairs playing pontoon with the former Education Minister, John Marcus O'Sullivan'. De Valera was duly elected Taoiseach and power was passed between the bitter foes.

EPILOGUE

It was Irish democracy's finest day and Cosgrave's finest hour. As J.J. Lee puts it in *Ireland 1912-1985*, 'nothing so became Cosgrave in office as his manner of leaving it.' Given what happened just a decade earlier, both sides did the new state a service by their behaviour during that 1932 campaign. A few years on, de Valera would pay the ultimate compliment to his bitter rivals. When his son Vivion was complaining about the 'Free-staters', he hushed him, saying: 'Yes, yes, we said all that, I know, I know. But when we got in and saw the files, they did a magnificent job, Viv. They did a magnificent job.'

42

Put Him In to Get Him Out
1917

PROLOGUE

May 1917 produced one of the most dramatic election results in Irish history. The South Longford by-election marked the death of the once-great Irish Parliamentary Party, with power being passed to Sinn Féin, which had emerged from the Easter Rising of a year earlier as, in the words of historian J.J. Lee, 'a popular-front resistance movement'. Sinn Féin had already won a by-election in Roscommon in February of that year, but Irish Party leader John Redmond put that down to a sympathy vote for its candidate Count Plunkett, father of the executed 1916 leader Joseph Mary Plunkett. South Longford seemed to be much less fertile territory for Sinn Féin than Roscommon. It was seen as a traditional heartland of the Irish Party.

There was huge reluctance about contesting the election from elements within Sinn Féin – notably Éamon de Valera and his fellow internees in Lewes Prison in Britain. They were resistant to efforts by Michael Collins to install Joe McGuinness, who was serving three years in Lewes for his role in the Easter Rising, as the Sinn Féin candidate. While they recognised the embarrassment a victory would cause to the British government, they had serious concerns that a defeat would reverse all the gains made since the Rising. They also had problems with the concept of acknowledging the British parliament. However, despite McGuinness's own serious misgivings, Collins went ahead and nominated him as the candidate, adopting the immortal slogan 'Put him in to get him out'. McGuinness's candidature meant that it would be the first time in 25 years that the constituency had a contested election.

With hindsight, Sinn Féin had many advantages going into the by-election. The reality was that the Irish Party had been in decline in Longford for some time and the party's cause was not helped by serious divisions in its camp. Infighting took place between the three prospective candidates and the person finally selected, Paddy McKenna, was late into the contest and did not enjoy the backing of all of his party. The Irish Party was also no match for Sinn Féin's formidable electoral machine. The challenger had more energy, more manpower, more colour – the constituency was covered with flags and posters – and more financial muscle.

In her book, *County Longford and the Irish Revolution*, Marie Coleman tells how 100 motorcars arrived from all over Ireland before election day to be used for Sinn Féin campaigning purposes, despite wartime restrictions on fuel. Party supporters in Castlerea contributed 42 precious tins of petrol and a car for the party's use. Every prominent Sinn Féiner not in prison was in the constituency addressing meetings.

It quickly became clear that Sinn Féin was attracting considerable support among young voters. Media reports appeared detailing how young men and women were refusing to do their duties on the farm or in the household unless their parents promised to support McGuinness. Although the Church hierarchy were mainly (though not exclusively as we will soon see) on the side of the Irish Party, young curates were openly supportive of Sinn Féin, even wearing their colours.

On the issues, Sinn Féin exploited fears that conscription would be introduced by the British government – claiming wrongly that Irish Party MPs would support it. More legitimately, they also highlighted the possibility of partition as part of the Home Rule settlement at the end of the war. And it was on this issue that the Dublin Archbishop William Walsh made a decisive entry into the election campaign.

Walsh, who had become increasingly disillusioned with the Irish Party and its methods, wrote a letter to the Dublin evening newspapers in which he condemned 'the partitionist' solution to home rule. He also suggested that the Irish Party had accepted partition, claiming that the 'country is practically sold'. Sinn Féin was relatively new to the whole election business, but not so new that it didn't know how to capitalise on the letter. They presented it as evidence to vote 'against the Irish Party traitors'.

THE DRAMA

While the campaign was exciting, it was nothing compared to the day of the count. The contest was incredibly tight. After the votes were counted, the returning officer in Longford courthouse announced a narrow victory for McKenna by just 12 votes. However, the combined votes received by both candidates fell well short of the total votes cast. A bundle of uncounted ballots was found and they pushed McGuinness 37 votes ahead of McKenna – 1,498 votes to 1,461. It was a sensational victory. The turnaround between the two announcements has spawned all sorts of stories and conspiracy theories. In his biography of Michael Collins, Tim Pat Coogan tells how Alasdair MacCaba, who went on to become a much-admired chairman of the Irish Educational Building Society, told him that after the first announcement: 'I jumped up on the platform, put a .45 to the head of the returning officer, clicked back the hammer and told him to "think again".'

Marie Coleman refers to this version of events in her book, but notes that it doesn't figure prominently in any other commentary on the election. She says that the more credible and probable account of how the result was overturned on a recount was given by Sinn Féin organiser Jack O'Sheehan in a letter to *The Sunday Press* many years later. In that letter, he credited Joe McGrath – future Sinn Féin TD, Cumann na nGaedheal minister and founder of the Irish Sweepstakes – with identifying a crucial counting error. Some 150 McGuinness votes had been pushed into a bundle only supposed to contain 100 votes. Coleman notes that this version of events is also contained in the memoirs of Irish Citizen Army member Joe Good.

EPILOGUE

The news of the Sinn Féin victory was signalled to the crowds waiting outside the courthouse by a man at the window unfurling a tricolour. The street outside erupted in jubilation, while bonfires burned on the hills. The result caused shockwaves across the Irish Sea, not least in Lewes Prison where McGuinness was carried shoulder high around the grounds of the prison to the amazement of warders.

It was a huge embarrassment for the British establishment. As Coleman puts it, a man in prison for treason was now elected as a parliamentary representative. *The Manchester Guardian* described it as 'the equivalent of a major British defeat in the field'. *The London Times* noted the trend of youth support for Sinn Féin, describing it as 'the most sinister portent of the South Longford election'. The pro-Irish Party media in Ireland blamed Archbishop Walsh's intervention. Given the tightness of the race, it was certainly a factor but the main reason for the result was the weak and divided Irish Party organisation, which had nothing to offer the electorate compared to the energy of Sinn Féin.

The result was devastating for the Irish Party. As Marie Coleman puts it, South Longford was 'a significant landmark in the eclipsing of the Irish Party by Sinn Féin as the dominant force in Irish politics'.

It was also, Coleman adds, vindication for those in Sinn Féin who advocated contesting elections – a policy that would bring big rewards. Two months later de Valera won a by-election in Clare and a year later the Irish Party was swept aside in the general election of 1918, winning just six seats compared to Sinn Féin's 73. A flag erected near Birr Castle after de Valera's victory summed up the Longford by-election's role in its demise: 'Irish Party – wounded in North Roscommon, killed in South Longford, buried in East Clare. RIP'.

McGuinness was subsequently returned in the elections of 1918 and 1921 and holds the unique record of being elected from prison on each occasion. However, the time he spent there took its toll on his health and he died in 1922 at just 57 years old.

The South Longford by-election, as well as providing political vindication for Michael Collins, also impacted on his personal life. Tim Pat Coogan recounts how, during the campaign, Collins stayed in The Greville Arms, run by the Kieran family. The story goes that Collins first fell in love with Helen Kieran. When she chose to marry another, the 'Big Fellow' famously transferred his affections to one of her sisters, Kitty, whom Collins's friend Harry Boland was already in love with – a fact, Coogan suggests, 'which may have had a bearing on his subsequent relationship with Collins.'

43

Tipp's Top Tory
1790

PROLOGUE

Brian O'Higgins' total of 114 first-preference votes is the lowest ever recorded for a successful Dáil candidate (see Chapter 27). However, by going further back in Irish political history, it's possible to find a future British prime minister who was elected with less than a quarter of that vote total. And unlike O'Higgins, he didn't need to get transfers from running mates to make it to parliament.

THE DRAMA

Two famous nineteenth century British prime ministers began their political careers in Ireland: Robert Peel and the Duke of Wellington (the latter was also born in Ireland). Arthur Wellesley, as he was known before becoming the legendary Duke of Wellington, sat as an MP for Trim between 1790 and 1797. He came from the established family of a nobleman who had lands in Trim and who 'owned' the seat in Trim. Wellesley gave up the seat in 1797 as he was serving overseas, later becoming a MP in two different English constituencies before becoming one of the leading figures in the House of Lords (which was at least as influential as the House of Commons at that time) and Prime Minister.

Peel began his parliamentary career in the 'pocket borough' of Cashel in 1809. The 21-year-old had just achieved a double first in classics and mathematics at Oxford and his mill-owning father rewarded his success – as highly influential fathers did in those days – by buying him the parliamentary seat of Cashel.

Wellesley, who by this stage was chief secretary of Ireland, sent a request to Cashel Corporation for Peel to be elected. He promised to 'let you know his Christian name by express tomorrow' – probably no bad thing, alright, to know the Christian name of the man you are going to elect. The Cashel seat cost the not-inconsiderable sum of £3,000 and it was bought from the Pennefather family, who between 1800 and 1810 provided mayors for the area in constant rotation.

There were 27 electors in Cashel and they tended to vote unanimously. The minutes of Cashel Corporation recorded: 'Pursuant to a precept directed to the Mayor of the City of Cashel from John Southcote Mansergh Esq., High Sheriff of the County of Tipperary (and great-great-great grandfather of former advisor to the Taoiseach and current TD for Tipperary South, Martin Mansergh), to elect and return him one proper person to represent this city in the Imperial Parliament, William Pennefather Mayor, after posting up notices in parts and places in the said city, when the Mayor, Bailiffs, Aldermen and Freemen assembled, [they] unanimously elected Robert Peel of Drayton Bassett and the county of Stafford Esq. to represent them in the said Imperial Parliament.' Such was the way in which MPs were elected in those far from democratic times.

Peel never visited the constituency and problems quickly

emerged with his new seat. It was Martin Mansergh, who had an obvious family interest in the story, who got to the bottom of what happened. He researched Peel's papers in the Library in Chequers, where the Irish delegation, of which he was part, was based during a break in Northern Ireland negotiations. Soon after Peel's election in 1809 with the first glimmer of ethics in government, legislation was passed making the sale of seats illegal, with a fine of £1,000.

In a review for *The Irish Times* of a biography of Peel, Manseragh noted that in 1812 Peel wrote to his new prime minister, Lord Liverpool (who Peel had previously served under as junior minister), that he had forsaken all thoughts of representing Cashel as 'I think the risk would be too great'. Instead, Peel's father paid in a roundabout way for a less notorious seat in Chippenham in England, which Peel represented from 1812 to 1817, and it would be 1829 before Peel would ever contest an election.

EPILOGUE

'Rotten boroughs' were far from unusual in Britain and Ireland in those days. The term generally referred to a constituency or borough which, due to its small size and tiny electorate, was controlled. Typically, they were boroughs which once had flourishing populations but which had become deserted over time.

The 'pocket borough' was one that had such a small electorate that it was in the control (or 'pocket') of a major landowner. At one point, three quarters of the MPs in the House of Commons were elected by less than 500 votes and while a place such as Old Sarum in Wiltshire, with three houses and 11 votes, had two MPs,

43 – Tipp's Top Tory

the entire city of Manchester had none. Many of the rotten boroughs were controlled by peers who established their sons in the seats to ensure influence in the House of Commons, while also holding seats themselves in the House of Lords.

Efforts were finally made to address the rotten boroughs, most notably in the Reform Act of 1832, which abolished 56 of them and created new seats in high-population areas. Pocket boroughs were finally abolished by the Reform Act of 1867, which established the principle that we have today whereby each constituency has roughly the same population per member of parliament.

44

Playing the Green Card
1982

PROLOGUE

The general election of November 1982 is one that Fianna Fáil does not like to be reminded about. After a half century of leaving an often hapless Fine Gael in its wake, the balance of power appeared to be firmly shifting. Charlie Haughey's disastrous GUBU government had collapsed after just eight months, plunging the country into its third general election campaign in less than 18 months. Given that public confidence had drained away from the government during its short, crisis-ridden tenure, this looked like an election Fianna Fáil simply couldn't win.

Haughey, who just a month earlier had survived another heave against him, was proving to be a serious electoral liability and the party remained badly divided over his leadership. Furthermore, it was up against a Fine Gael party that knew exactly what it was doing. Its leader, Garret FitzGerald, was popular with the electorate and the traditional gap in organisation and public relations between the two main parties had been firmly closed. In fact, for probably the first time in its history, Fine Gael was way ahead in this regard.

The party's new slick, professional approach – overseen by its strategy committee, largely made up of businessmen – was typified by its very sharp and hard-hitting television advertising. Probably the best remembered of the ads juxtaposed dissident Fianna Fáil deputies with those loyal to Haughey to the sound of Frank Sinatra singing *Love and Marriage* (with particular emphasis on the line 'You can't have one without the other').

The first opinion poll of the campaign was disastrous for Fianna Fáil. For the first time ever the two main parties were equal in support (42 per cent each), with Labour's 8 per cent putting the opposition combination well ahead. FitzGerald was 1 – 3 with the bookies to lead the next government. They were desperate times for Haughey and Fianna Fáil, and desperate times often produce desperate measures.

THE DRAMA

Exactly two weeks before polling day, Fianna Fáil, with no aces left in its pack, opted to play the 'Green Card'. The party baldly accused FitzGerald of allowing himself to be used as an instrument of British policy in Ireland. The accusation was based on a story in a British newspaper. The story suggested that FitzGerald had been used by the British Secretary of State for Northern Ireland, Jim Prior, to lobby the Duke of Norfolk, a Catholic peer in the House of Lords, in support of Prior's devolution proposals for the North.

Rejecting the allegation as false, FitzGerald said that he did meet the Duke the previous July, but the only matter on which he had lobbied him was against the British government's exclusion of the candidature of SDLP deputy leader Seamus Mallon from the revived Northern Assembly because he was a member of the

Seanad.

However, in politics (and particularly in the heat of an election battle) perception is everything. Fianna Fáil went for the jugular. Foreign Affairs Minister Gerry Collins challenged FitzGerald to say how many other British politicians he had approached on Prior's behalf.

The following day at a press conference, the Taoiseach Charlie Haughey told Britain to keep out of Ireland's election. According to Bruce Arnold's book, *What Kind of Country*, Haughey suggested that British radio, television and certain Fleet Street newspapers were interfering in Irish affairs. He implied that Fianna Fáil was being attacked by the British media, motivated by the British establishment, as a result of the 'independent' stance Ireland had adopted during Britain's war with Argentina over the Falklands.

Later that night at a party rally in Trim, County Meath, Haughey went further, claiming the issue on which the election 'turned' was Ireland's sovereignty and independence. 'The Irish people asserted their sovereign right to independence in the past, and today they must reassert that right. I am once again saying, as I said at a press conference earlier today, that we want the British to stay out of the election. We arranged their departure from our country 60 years ago, and we don't want them coming back in 1982. We want a resounding victory in this election as an indication of your support for the freedom and independence of Ireland as a whole.'

Less than a week later, Fianna Fáil was given fresh ammunition. With FitzGerald due to give his one election speech on the North, Jim Prior was reported as stating at a Washington press conference that the Fine Gael leader would shortly be proposing an all-Ireland court and an all-Ireland police force.

As FitzGerald later put it in *All in a Life*, this scarcely showed great prescience, as he made that very suggestion to an audience of several million people in the BBC Dimbleby Lecture the previous May and Prior had been in the audience.

Fianna Fáil used the comments to attack FitzGerald on two fronts. Firstly, they bluntly accused FitzGerald of collusion with the British government and of Fine Gael collaboration which, it said, amounted to the 'most serious threat to the Republic of Ireland's independence since the Second World War'.

As well as portraying FitzGerald as a puppet of the British, they also presented Fine Gael's position on an all-Ireland police force as a plan to have the likes of Kerry and Donegal policed by the RUC.

This, of course, was patent nonsense. Firstly, the proposed force would be separate from both the Garda Síochána and the RUC; secondly, the British weren't keen on any all-Ireland institution (so the idea was never likely to see the light of day); and thirdly, Fianna Fáil itself had supported the idea of an all-Ireland court. But there is little doubt that for pragmatic political reasons, FitzGerald would have been better off steering clear of the issue during election time – a view shared by many in Fine Gael at the time.

Haughey, fighting for his political life, was not going to pass up on the opportunity. He said on radio that the 'British government and Mr Prior are actively intervening in our internal affairs and trying to influence this election'. Asked if he was playing the 'Green Card', Haughey replied: 'If it involves asserting Ireland's right to independence, to run our own affairs without interference from the British, if that is playing the Green Card, yes, I am playing it,' adding, 'Britain, stay out of our election.'

While FitzGerald has argued that the controversy did not impact much on his party's support on polling day, there is little doubt that it had, to quote Bruce Arnold, 'an immediate and adverse impact on the Fine Gael campaign.' However, as Arnold also pointed out, it was defused somewhat by FitzGerald's calm dismissal of the claims, the actual speech he did deliver the following Thursday evening on the North, and Haughey's 'patent over-reaction'.

Fianna Fáil continued to play the Green Card in the final days of the campaign, which were marked by bitterness and hostility, with relations further deteriorating between Haughey and FitzGerald. The latter claimed Haughey was waging a campaign of lies and vilification against him, to which Haughey responded that he had told no lies, adding: 'I have only made attacks on his policies and his actions.'

Campaigning in the two marginal constituencies of Kerry, Haughey had strongly emphasised the British connection with Fine Gael. He then returned to Dublin for a press briefing on the Saturday before polling day, where he insisted that in meeting the Duke of Norfolk, FitzGerald had lunched with a 'trained British spy'; the Duke's CV, identifying him as head of intelligence at the British Ministry of Defence, was produced as evidence.

Leaflets were produced in some constituencies asking: 'Do you want the RUC policing our streets?', along with others suggesting British Prime Minister Margaret Thatcher 'needed' FitzGerald. There was talk of FitzGerald grabbing defeat from the jaws of victory and a widespread view that the all-Ireland police force would cost his party votes and, potentially, seats in border constituencies. An opinion poll, taken a week before election day, showed a narrowing of the gap (with Fianna Fáil gaining ground in Connacht–Ulster), but still indicated that combined support for Fine Gael and Labour was well ahead.

Bruce Arnold has argued that FitzGerald successfully challenged Fianna Fáil's 'lurch into verbal republicanism' head on, firstly by discrediting Haughey's accusations one by one in a critical and widely reported radio interview, and secondly, by making a point of attending a function held by the British–Irish Association – a 'provocative public endorsement by FitzGerald of where he stood in terms of British–Irish relations'.

Arnold also argues, with some merit, that for perhaps the first time in any general election, 'the traditional verbal republicanism of Fianna Fáil, which sought an undefined, eventual unity of Ireland, without spelling out the intermediate actions designed to achieve that goal, was being challenged by a man whose credentials offered the best alternative in terms of policy and commitment': in layman's language, a facing down of the old fireside republicanism that achieved nothing by the type of practical, open-to-compromise partnership approach that would, for example, deliver the 1985 Anglo-Irish Agreement (heavily backed by the electorate) and, years later, the Northern Ireland peace process.

EPILOGUE

In the end the Green Card, like any tactic of desperation, was doomed to failure. There is a view that Haughey erred in publishing a book of estimates six days out from polling day, which not only sparked public criticism because of the planned cutbacks, but also interrupted 'the Green Card stoking of anti-British feelings which had become a significant, if geographically mixed, asset' (Bruce Arnold).

But the critical factor was that Haughey and Fianna Fáil's credibility problem, after eight disastrous and divisive months in government, was simply insurmountable.

In the leaders' debate, held just 36 hours before the polls opened (see Chapter 20), Haughey surprisingly did not raise the allegations of collusion and collaboration. He did accuse FitzGerald of proposing 'a British-Irish police force' to police Ireland. But he was faced down by the Fine Gael leader, who handed him his speech and asked him to point out where there was a reference to a 'British-Irish force'. Haughey took the script but declined to pursue the issue.

FitzGerald won the debate and the election. Fine Gael took 70 seats and almost 40 per cent of the vote, and with Labour's surprisingly good performance of 16 seats (see Chapter 37) secured a comfortable majority. Coming within five seats of Fianna Fáil's total, it seemed as if finally it was on the verge of taking its mantle as the natural party of government.

Given how badly the election had gone for Fianna Fáil and how strong Fine Gael looked, nobody could have predicted that over the following quarter of a century, Fine Gael would fail to win even one of the next six general elections.

45

Reds Under the Bed
1932 – 1969

PROLOGUE

For a country that has given only negligible support to the Communist Party, produced a mere handful of TDs who could ever be regarded as communist and has never really had a left–right divide like most other European countries, it is remarkable how often the 'Red Scare' has been used in Irish general elections. In fact, it was not just in Irish elections. In the late 1940s, after the de-facto Soviet takeover of Central and Eastern Europe, the Archbishop of Dublin, Charles McQuaid, made a personal appeal on Radio Éireann – with the full approval of the inter-party government – for funds to help defeat the communists in the upcoming general election in Italy.

Whatever about in Italy, where the Communist Party was traditionally strong, the search for 'Reds under the bed' in Irish politics was a lot more challenging. Not that this stopped the main political parties from looking.

THE DRAMA

Act I

In the general election of 1932, the Cumann na nGaedheal government was under serious pressure from the vibrant new Fianna Fáil party. Tired after ten years in government and devoid of ideas in comparison with the hungry main opposition party, Cumann na nGaedheal opted for negative campaigning. The party, as J.J. Lee put it, 'based its platform squarely on law, order, religion and the "Red scare". It tried to co-opt the Catholic church as a honourary party agent.'

Cumann na nGaedheal painted Fianna Fáil as a party of extremists that would give a free hand to communists and terrorists; in other words, electing Fianna Fáil to power would lead to another civil war. In one newspaper advertisement the government party claimed, 'The gunmen are voting Fianna Fáil; the communists are voting Fianna Fáil'. A poster showed a red flag superimposed on a tricolour and stated: 'We want no Reds, keep their colour off your Flag.' Another warned that, 'You cannot afford to take a chance ... with communism'. Éamon de Valera's accession to power would endanger the lives of peaceful citizens and the rights of farmers to their land, the propaganda warned.

Cumann na nGaedheal, in comparison, would 'shelter our national heritage from doctrines which are subversive of religion, home and country'. But a Fianna Fáil victory would bring irreligion and transform Ireland 'into a field for the cultivation of those doctrines of materialism and communism which can so effectively poison the wells of religion and national traditions.' The government claimed that the country's place 'in the community of nations, the recognition we have received from the Holy Father and the principal powers of the world . . . will disappear with the destruction of the state.'

Despite it being patently obvious that de Valera and his party were not communists who 'received dictation from Moscow', Fianna Fáil felt compelled to deny that its members had leanings towards communism. In a speech during the campaign, Seán Lemass insisted that Fianna Fáil policy was not related to communism, but was a constructive alternative to it. 'Not all the Russian gold in the world could produce communism [in Ireland] unless in consequence of unemployment and bad housing, resulting from government neglect,' he added pointedly.

Whether or not the Cumann na nGaedheal scare tactics had any impact on voters is difficult to ascertain. It was certainly, as J.J. Lee has pointed out, a 'sure sign of conceptual bankruptcy'. It may arguably have limited the drop in its own vote, but it certainly did not stop the party losing power. Fianna Fáil gained 15 seats, while the government's vote dropped and it lost 5 seats. De Valera was elected President of the Executive Council, and he stayed there for much of the next 27 years with 'ne'er a sign of communists' in his governments in all that time.

Act II

Despite what happened to them in 1932, Fianna Fáil was not shy about later playing the Red card. And the man mainly dealing the pack was Seán MacEntee, one of the party's most senior politicians in the first three decades of its existence. MacEntee was known for his great personal charm and warmth, but the Belfast-born man had no difficulty removing the gloves when entering the political arena.

In the 1943 general election, MacEntee declared in a leaflet that 'even in these most dangerous days when the nation should be firmly united, the Labour Party seeks to set class against class'. He publicly alleged 'communist infiltration' of Labour, citing the communist past of Jim Larkin (newly returned to the Labour fold) and claiming that Larkin's son – also a candidate – was 'Moscow trained'.

Three years later in the three by-elections of October 1947, MacEntee noted that Labour leader William Norton had recently been threatening a general strike: 'the weapon mostly commonly adopted by the communists on their march to power.'

Those by-elections saw the emergence of a new left-wing republican party, Clann na Poblachta, that was soon regarded as a huge threat to Fianna Fáil. The run-up to polling day saw an extraordinarily sharp exchange of letters in *The Irish Press* between MacEntee and leader Seán MacBride who was contesting the Dublin County by-election.

In a strong and highly personalised attack, MacEntee pointed out that one of MacBride's close associates in Clann na Poblachta was a founder of 'the Vanguard', whose aim was the destruction of capitalism, the establishment of a socialist republic and its ultimate absorption into a European federation of socialist republics. MacEntee also brought up MacBride's past links to the IRA and Saor Éire (a short-lived left-wing nationalist group regarded by the bishops as 'communistic in its aims'), and claimed that members of Clann na Poblachta didn't serve in the defence forces during the 'Emergency' (the Second World War). MacBride, not unreasonably, pointed out that his past links to the IRA were no more relevant than MacEntee's or anybody else's in Fianna Fáil.

At an election speech in Clonmel for the Tipperary by-election that October, MacEntee warned that these were critical days in

Europe. The communist organisation, with their roots and headquarters in Moscow, had received orders to foment civil strife and revolution in those countries of Western Europe where democracy still prevailed. They had placed agents, he said, in trade unions, labour movements and in militant and left-wing organisations (no prizes for guessing which ones). He then went on to present what *The Irish Press* described as 'detailed evidence', showing that men prominently associated with Clann na Poblachta and Labour in the by-election campaigns had been 'used' by a secret communist organisation in this country. The leaders of Clann na Poblachta were 'a grave menace to the national and Christian principles of Irish people'. MacBride responded that his party wanted 'a state, not merely Christian in name, but in fact'. Another senior party figure assured voters there was 'no communism and no fascism in Clann na Poblachta. There is no "ism" of any kind but Irish-ism,' he said.

At an eve of by-election rally in Dublin, MacEntee was shouted down and responded, 'So much for free speech, the sort people of Moscow believe in.' And in a swipe aimed at Clann na Poblachta, who were trying to drown him out, he told them the only reason they were there was because their friends in Nazi Germany had lost the war – a reference to the IRA's support for the Nazi war effort (although MacBride had left the IRA in 1937).

MacEntee warned that given the dangers in Europe, Ireland could not afford to overthrow a great and experienced leader for those like MacBride and his friends who did not even rally to the nation 'in those days of trial'.

However, despite MacEntee's rhetoric, MacBride won the by-election in Dublin County and his party Clann na Poblachta also won in Tipperary – a sensational result for the new party.

Act III

Fianna Fáil was rattled by the by-election defeats and de Valera opted to go to the country early in 1948 to try to head off the rising Clann. The latter, not without foundation, accused Fianna Fáil of deliberately calling the election before the introduction of a new electoral register that would have given the vote to thousands of new voters. The election saw Fianna Fáil 'continuing the same abortive "Red scare"' tactics against Labour and Clann na Poblachta that Seán MacEntee had so enthusiastically pursued in the October by-elections,' wrote J.J. Lee. It was certainly not for the faint-hearted as Fianna Fáil and the Clann, in particular, tore strips off each other. They both sensed the country wasn't big enough for the two of them – Fianna Fáil, in particular, was determined it wasn't going to be shoved aside by these radical republican newcomers.

MacEntee (who else?) repeatedly stated that the Labour Party was 'riddled' with communists, but most of his attacks seemed to be focused on Clann na Poblachta. He once again raised MacBride's past in Saor Éire and in leading the 'Red IRA', recalling a series of atrocities the organisation had been involved in during the 1930s and claiming that senior figures now in Clann na Poblachta had tried to 'promote a state of disorder' during the Emergency. In yet another letter to *The Irish Press*, MacEntee said it was well known that members of the national executive of the Clann and Labour were frequent visitors to a bookshop on Pearse Street (which was one of the locations in Dublin where – shock, horror – communists were secretly working). Furthermore, he said, a well-known figure in the Labour Party – the person was not a TD – 'held court' in a school on Harcourt Street where lectures on issues such as Marxism and socialism were given.

MacEntee also questioned whether MacBride was ever a

nationalist at all, suggesting all he wanted was an 'Irish state after the model of Red Russia'.

It is telling that Clann na Poblachta were sufficiently worried about the 'Red scare' tactics that they ran advertisements in the newspapers declaring that 'there are no communists in Clann na Poblachta', stressing the party's Christian principles and promising it would not adopt communist or fascist ideas or methods. A senior member, Peadar Cowan – formerly of the Labour Party – felt compelled to declare that he was 'not a communist' after allegations from MacEntee.

Similarly, Labour Party leader William Norton felt the need to declare that his party would 'use all its strength to ensure that communism will not stain the political and religious life of the Irish people'.

However, as with Cumann na nGaedheal in 1932, negative campaigning and smears were to prove no substitute for real policies and fresh ideas. Fianna Fáil, with the help of a well-thought-out boundary revision (see Chapter 32), succeeded in limiting Clann na Poblachta to just ten seats. It was a hugely disappointing performance for the new party that had hoped to at least overtake Fine Gael and become the second biggest party. But a combination of too many candidates, poor tactics and overconfidence, allied to the boundary changes and, perhaps, the aggressive Fianna Fáil tactics, restricted the Clann to 7 per cent of the Dáil seats and 13 per cent of the vote.

However, while the threat of being outflanked by Clann na Poblachta was seen off, Fianna Fáil did not have a good election. It lost eight seats and – after being in power for 16 years – was replaced by the state's first inter-party government, which included the two (far from) 'communist' parties of Labour and Clann na Phoblachta, as well as Fine Gael, National Labour and Clann na

Talmhan. Not surprisingly, the bitterness of the campaign caused serious tensions between party supporters at rallies.

At the count in Rathmines Town Hall, where MacBride was declared elected, having topped the poll in Dublin South West, there were also ugly scenes. Successful Fianna Fáil candidate Bernard Butler had to be escorted from the hall by gardaí. He had spoken about placards being torn down and general dirty tricks by opposition supporters in his victory speech, but was interrupted by a man who approached him shouting: 'Do you believe Clann na Poblachta are communistic [sic]?' Significantly, MacBride himself paid tribute to the way Labour and Fine Gael had conducted their campaigns, but said he would remain silent as to his other opponents.

Act IV

But it wasn't just Fianna Fáil politicians who played the 'Red card' at this time. The decision to re-admit long-time dissident Jim Larkin and his son, Jim Junior, as official candidates for the 1943 general election did not just provide ammunition for Seán MacEntee: it caused a serious split in the Labour Party itself. Both Larkins were successful in that election, but there had been strenuous opposition to their re-admission to the party from Larkin's old enemy William O'Brien, head of the ITGWU – the union Larkin had founded in 1908. The following January, the ITGWU disaffiliated from the Labour Party on the grounds of 'communist infiltration'. Five of the eight Labour TDs who were members of that union left the party to establish National Labour. The new party declared that it was 'irrevocably committed to the Papal encyclicals'.

Labour responded to the allegation of communist infiltration by firmly denying it and by setting up a commission of inquiry, under leader William Norton, who said that 'nobody will be allowed to masquerade as a member of the Labour Party with the object of promoting communism'. The commission investigated 17 prominent left-wingers and six party members were expelled from Labour in April 1944. The timing of the breakaway by National Labour couldn't have been worse for Labour which, having trebled its vote since the dark days of 1933, seemed to be on the up. Instead, not for the last time, the party proceeded to tear itself apart. O'Brien, according to J.J. Lee, 'ran a "Red scare"' campaign against Labour, gleefully abetted by Fianna Fáil, especially [surprise, surprise] Seán MacEntee.'

De Valera responded to the split in Labour by seizing the opportunity to call a fresh election in May 1944. Neither Labour party fared well. 'Old' Labour won just eight seats, while National Labour took four – compared with 17 for Labour just a year earlier. The squabble had cost Labour all the gains it had made in the 1943 general election – the 'Red Scare' tactics certainly didn't help – and it would be another seven years before the two parties would unite again.

Act V

The 1969 general election is probably the one best remembered for 'Red Scare' tactics. Some would say that the Labour Party was asking for trouble with its 'the '70s will be socialist' slogan – Fianna Fáil certainly thought so. It regarded Labour as the real danger in that election and it seemed to have good reason. The party was putting up 99 candidates – more than twice the number of 1965 – and they included high-profile intellectuals such as Conor Cruise O'Brien, Noel Browne, David Thornley and Justin Keating, along with UCD economics lecturer John O'Donovan. The presence of these candidates ensured massive media

45 – Reds Under the Bed

coverage. Ruling out coalition with either of the two 'civil-war parties', Labour insisted its ambition was to form a single-party government and it ran a highly professional and modern campaign.

But it was no match for Fianna Fáil when it came to street fighting. J.J. Lee wrote that Fianna Fáil leader Jack Lynch 'seized the opportunity offered by Labour's careless socialist rhetoric to play a "Red scare" hand with a velvet touch that Seán MacEntee must have envied.' But while Lynch undoubtedly used a velvet touch, some of those under him opted to go straight for the jugular. An early Fianna Fáil advertisement described Labour's policies as 'alien doctrines which are foreign to our people's traditions and beliefs'.

Director of Elections Charlie Haughey explained that Fianna Fáil would not be issuing a manifesto because 'manifestos have a Marxist ring about them'; there was little doubt as to what, or who, he was getting at. Other individuals went further. Local Government Minister Kevin Boland claimed Labour wanted to seize people's land, property and savings. Justice Minister Michael Moran said Labour leader Brendan Corish was a 'mere puppet of the modern Marxist elite and of the new left-wing political queers who have taken over the Labour Party from the steps of Trinity College and Telefís Éireann'. There was even a claim that Labour would 'confiscate' the Guinness Brewery – as historian Dermot Ferriter recently put it, 'in the interests of socialism rather than sobriety.'

Another minister, Neil Blaney, said Labour membership 'ranged from capitalists to pseudo-intellectual Marxists, Maoists, Trotskyites and the like who have emerged from the sidelines like carrion birds to pick off the flesh of Irish people'. Seán MacEntee, no doubt anxious not to be left out, claimed Labour stood for

Lenin, Stalin and 'the Red flames of burning homesteads in Meath'.

During the previous Labour party conference, Cruise O'Brien had made a passing comment to the effect that Ireland should close its diplomatic mission in Portugal (then of course not a democracy) and open one in Cuba. Now every attack from Fianna Fáil included an allusion to Castro or Cuba. Labour, it claimed, wanted to impose Cuban socialism on Ireland. Taoiseach Jack Lynch asked whether land nationalisation was 'still' among Labour's policies.

There were also implicit accusations of anti-Catholicism or atheism against Labour. Defence Minister Michael Hilliard said some of those who had forced their way into Labour's ranks were 'not believers in fundamental Christian principles'. A Fianna Fáil candidate in Mayo famously said that with a Labour government, laws permitting abortion and divorce would be brought in and it would be 'great for the fellow who wanted a second wife every night'. One Labour TD alleged that Fianna Fáil was claiming in his constituency that Labour policy would be to throw priests in prison. In Sligo it was alleged that it was Labour policy to tear down every crucifix in the country.

Labour believed that in Lynch's tour of the country's convents – yes, the Taoiseach of the day used to drop into convents in the various towns he was visiting on his campaign –the Fianna Fáil leader was portraying the Labour party as dangerously extremist. There were allegations that the nuns were telling pupils in convent schools to inform their parents not to vote Labour.

Labour didn't take the insults lying down: one candidate in Tipperary retorted by questioning whether 'Tacaism [a reference to Fianna Fáil's fundraising organisation of 500 businessmen] was more Irish and Christian than socialist'. Senior party figures recalled that 'Red scare' tactics had been tried against Irish patriots before and that the capitalist policies of the two main parties had been derived from British imperialism.

However, in rural areas, many Labour deputies hardly mentioned their Labour connection at all during the campaign. In places such as Kerry North, the "70s will be socialist' posters were left behind lock and key. The party also emphasised that it was Christian socialist, with leader Brendan Corish stating that the policies were in line with encyclicals of the late Pope John XXIII.

Labour did significantly gain votes in the election, recording its highest percentage vote since 1922. The party did well in Dublin, with the intellectual high-fliers making it to the Dáil. But the overall result was a loss of four seats – down to 18. The party lost many of its old rural seats, including two TDs of twenty years' standing, where its radical policies simply did not attract support. Given that the party was at one point talking about single-party government, the result, to quote Trinity's Michael Gallagher in his book on the Irish Labour Party, was 'traumatically disappointing'.

The enduring image of RTÉ's election-night coverage was of a shattered-looking Brendan Corish at the count in Wexford asking Jack Lynch (sitting in studio) where in the party's policy documents was there anything 'alien to Christian beliefs'. Lynch was unmoved, retorting that the 'extreme form of socialism' Labour had been 'preaching' was 'an anathema to the Irish people'. He may have had a point.

As Gallagher noted, the fact that a smear campaign was conducted was beyond dispute. But he also posed the question as to whether Labour had left itself vulnerable to such attacks by its unrealistic predictions of socialist government and inexperienced candidates. There were shortcomings in the Labour campaign, and it certainly seems that the party tried to do too much too soon.

To form a single-party government, it would have needed to gain 60 new TDs, the majority of whom would be unknowns. It had a big credibility problem.

It is hard to know just how big an impact the Red smear had. As Gallagher points out, it's difficult to believe that the Irish electorate gave too much credence to the stories about destroying crucifixes and imprisoning priests. But the allegations that Labour would nationalise land must have done the party damage outside Dublin.

Recalling the Fianna Fáil smear tactics years later on the RTÉ documentary *Lights, Camera, Farrell*, Labour's general secretary at the time, Brendan Halligan, said their impact has been 'strongly underestimated by subsequent historians . . . they were nasty and they were meant to be and they were meant to damage us, which they did'.

Halligan added: 'It was done very skilfully. What was happening in the parlours of various convents throughout the country is something that we'll never discover, but we can only suspect . . . what happened over the rattle of the tea cups.'

He also recalled the story of a parish priest in a particular part of the country at the time explaining that the difference between socialism and communism was that socialism was a 'sort of Protestant communism'. Socialism, by that reckoning, was even worse than communism!

EPILOGUE

While it is true that we never had a full-blown, high-profile McCarthy-style communist witch-hunt in this country – possibly because the threat from communism was so small – all of the main parties in Dáil Éireann have had to defend themselves from allegations of communist sympathies. Even Fine Gael leader James Dillon, who once taunted Labour for trying to turn Ireland into the 'Cuba of the Atlantic', was forced to deny his own party consisted of 'Bolshevik revolutionaries' – presumably a reference to the liberal wing of Fine Gael that came up with the 'Just Society' programme.

The fall of the Berlin Wall in 1989 has rendered 'Red scare' tactics very much redundant. Immediately before the 2007 general election campaign, Taoiseach Bertie Ahern dismissed the proposed alternative coalition as a 'whole lot of parties that would be probably green and red, and maybe even redder'. But nobody particularly noticed.

A couple of years earlier, when Ahern described himself as a socialist, the nation collectively chuckled at the very notion. There were comical and satirical conversations in Dáil Éireann about who were the remaining socialists in the house. Socialism was defunct. It was all very different from the mid-1960s when Jack McQuillan – once of Clann na Poblachta, but by then a Labour TD for Roscommon – felt he had to sue a local newspaper for reporting a councillor's allegation that he was a communist. The All-Ireland medal-holder said he was a practising Catholic and if the allegation gained credence his whole career 'might be endangered'. The jury found in his favour but awarded only a halfpenny in damages. McQuillan lost his seat in the 1965 general election.

46

The Day Mickey Doherty Took a Pfennig off the Pound

1992

PROLOGUE

It was the end of November 1992, and Fianna Fáil was enduring its worst general election result in over sixty years. It had been a disastrous election campaign for Taoiseach Albert Reynolds and Fianna Fáil. Seat losses were expected but nobody had thought the result would be this bad. With Labour's Spring Tide swamping everybody else, Fianna Fáil was heading for just 68 seats – down nine and an unthinkable low for the 'natural party' of government.

While the election was going on, a full-blown currency crisis was taking place in the EU's Exchange Rate Mechanism (ERM). The previous September Britain had taken Sterling out of the ERM on 'Black Wednesday', following intensive pressure on the pound from currency speculators, and the Spanish and Portuguese had been subsequently forced to devalue their currencies. Speculators quickly turned their attention to the Irish pound.

For reasons that were a lot clearer at the time, the government fought a desperate rearguard action to stave off the speculators and avoid a devaluation. In the end, the government's strategy was doomed to failure and the price paid for this desperate rearguard (very high interest rates) was costly.

Meanwhile, back at the ranch (Albert's supporters were known as the 'country and western' wing of the party), Reynolds – understandably enough – was taking the election result very badly. In his book *The Power Game*, Stephen Collins wrote that the Taoiseach, at home in Longford for the count, literally 'took to the bed' for a few hours.

THE DRAMA

Mickey Doherty, Reynolds' election agent, tried to explain the Taoiseach's absence from the count by saying the Taoiseach was engaged in urgent consultations about the Irish pound. According to *The Power Game*, 'journalists reported the comments on the wire services and the Irish pound dropped by a couple of pfennig against the German mark. Sean Duignan [Reynolds' government press secretary] has famously told the story as "the day Mickey Doherty took a pfennig off the pound".'

In his book on his days as press secretary, *One Spin on the Merry-Go-Round*, Duignan refers to the incident, quoting from the diary he kept: 'Mickey Doherty announces a cabinet meeting on currency crisis tomorrow (doing his best to explain away Albert's late arrival at the count), causing all kinds of panic on the international exchanges – "Jaysus, Mickey," sez someone, "you've taken two effing phennigs off the mark!" which is true!'

EPILOGUE

Albert Reynolds was able to grab victory from the jaws of defeat, but there was to be no reprieve for the punt. According to *The*

Power Game, it was Sean Doherty, the controversial former Minister for Justice, who forced his way into Albert's bedroom on the day of the count to tell him to snap out of it. Reynolds, blessed with a naturally sunny disposition, did just that and was quickly talking about the possibility of linking up with Labour. Nobody else thought it would happen but within weeks Reynolds had stunned everybody by doing a deal with Dick Spring to form a Fianna Fáil–Labour coalition. Although Fianna Fáil bucked the election result, to quote Margaret Thatcher, there was to be no 'bucking the markets', and the Irish pound was devalued by 10% at the end of January 1993.

It was regarded almost as a blow to our national prestige at the time, but within a few years the Celtic Tiger was the toast of the Western world. If anything the devaluation helped our economic development. But long after the devaluation is forgotten, the day Mickey Doherty took a pfennig off the Irish pound will be fondly remembered.

47

George 'Second Best' (Dublin Central – 2)
1981 – 1987

PROLOGUE

Bertie Ahern needs little introduction. As a national politician, he has achieved it all. He has been the second longest serving Taoiseach in the history of the State, he was an acclaimed president of the EU for a six-month period, he turned down the prestigious job of president of the European Commission and he was a minister for finance under both Charlie Haughey and Albert Reynolds. But Ahern has never forgotten the importance of local politics. Even as Taoiseach, it's not unusual to see him canvassing his constituency on a Saturday afternoon though it might be at least a couple of years away from an election.

His legendary Dublin Central political machine is based in his St Luke's constituency office in the heart of Drumcondra and the people who are part of his inner circle have been dubbed the 'Drumcondra mafia'. Funding comes from an annual dinner held in Kilmainham Hospital and, more recently, in Clontarf Castle. Ahern was first elected to the Dáil for Dublin Finglas in 1977, coming in behind running mate Jim Tunney. However, a redrawing of the boundaries in the wake of that election saw Dublin Central re-established as a separate constituency – it has been Ahern's constituency ever since.

47 – George 'Second Best' (Dublin Central – 2)

In nine general elections since 1977, Ahern has topped the poll and never once failed to exceed the quota with his first-preference vote – an extraordinary achievement, particularly given some of the opposition he has had to face in that time. Of all the big names he has overcome, George Colley stands out. Colley was Charles Haughey's rival for the leadership from the mid 1960s to the early 1980s; a man who served as both Tánaiste and Minister for Finance but who was narrowly beaten by Haughey in the 1979 leadership contest. Such was Colley's strength in Fianna Fáil and the depth of his opposition to Haughey, he initially held a veto over Haughey's appointments to key cabinet positions such as Defence and Justice.

When Dublin Central was re-established for the February 1981 general election, the assumption must have been that Colley, then Tánaiste, would be the top dog in the constituency. But Ahern, who was very firmly in the Haughey camp, had other ideas. No doubt to Haughey's delight, it was Ahern who topped the poll in Dublin Central in that election, although Colley was also elected on the first count. Eight months later, in the February 1982 election, Ahern again topped the poll, with a slightly bigger margin over Colley. Haughey made him chief whip in his minority government. Colley, in turn, was told by Haughey that he would not be made Tánaiste and, as a result, refused to serve in cabinet. The balance of power between Ahern and Colley had shifted not just locally, but in national politics. However, by that stage Colley was still seen by many as the leader of the anti-Haughey faction, although within Fianna Fáil Des O'Malley was becoming more prominent.

Haughey survived a motion of no confidence, put down out of the blue by Charlie McCreevy, the following October. But within weeks, his crisis-ridden government – forever to be remembered as the GUBU government – fell. The defeat on a motion of no confidence meant a third general election in 18 months. So many elections in such a short time hardly helped alleviate tensions between the Ahern and Colley camps in Dublin Central, to put it mildly. The election was seen as crucial by Colley supporters. With Fianna Fáil likely to lose power, a strong performance would be helpful to Colley if he was to challenge Haughey's leadership afterwards. Bertie Ahern, however, had other plans.

THE DRAMA

There was bitter rivalry between the Ahern and Colley camps during the November 1982 general election. In many ways Dublin Central was a proxy Fianna Fáil leadership contest with Ahern representing the Haughey wing and Colley the so-called 'Club of 22' that had voted against Haughey the previous month. The tensions came to a head on polling day with open hostility on the streets of the constituency between supporters from the Ahern and Colley camps. Both camps were represented at most polling stations in the constituency, with *The Irish Times* reporting that one group handed out 'leaflets on behalf of the official Fianna Fáil slate while the other group stood some distance away, openly canvassing only for Mr Colley'.

At the Malborough Street polling station in the heart of the capital, the tensions spilled over into 'a brawl between the rival groups, after a Fianna Fáil official attempted to take the pro-Colley literature away from one of the former Tánaiste's supporters. According to one eyewitness, the Colley canvasser was 'dragged to the ground while an attempt was made to strip him of the offending leaflets', with the report adding that less serious confrontations between the two factions were also witnessed at other polling stations. The faction fight apparently followed the circulation of leaflets to electors in the constituency calling on them to support Ahern, but making no mention of Colley or Tom Leonard, the third Fianna Fáil candidate. 'This was clearly an attempt by the Ahern camp to screw George Colley,' one of Colley's supporters was quoted as saying. Colley, in turn, had circulated leaflets telling voters that he needed every vote to secure re-election. Unlike Ahern's leaflets, Colley's literature did go on to call for support for the other two Fianna Fáil candidates. And the pro-Colley people told *The Irish Times* that the decision to issue their letter had been taken 'very reluctantly' and only in response to 'massive intimidation' from the Ahern camp.

Unfortunately for Colley, the result this time around was even more emphatic. Ahern secured almost twice as many votes as Colley; in fact, his vote total increased by 2,000 votes, whilst Colley's decreased by almost the same amount. Despite the bitter rivalry between the two camps, over 1,800 of Ahern's votes transferred to Colley, ensuring he was elected on the second count. But there was now no doubting who was king in Dublin Central.

EPILOGUE

Within a few months, there would be no doubt who was boss in Fianna Fáil either, although it was touch and go for Haughey for a short while. The rise in Ahern's vote bucked the national trend with Fianna Fáil having a disastrous election and Fine Gael and Labour securing an overall majority. Revelations soon emerged about the tapping of journalists' phones and Fianna Fáil was plunged into another crisis. At one point, it seemed certain that Haughey's days as leader were over, but he fought a tenacious battle, winning over wavering deputies, and just about survived as leader. After that the anti-Haughey faction, no doubt exhausted after the stresses and strains of the previous three years, disintegrated. A number of them had lost their seats the previous November. Within two years, Haughey's main rival, Des O'Malley, had been expelled from the party. Later that year, O'Malley established the PDs, bringing with him a number of those who had opposed Haughey. For the first time since he had become leader in 1979, Haughey was now in complete control of his party. Sadly, that November 1982 general election was to prove George Colley's last. Within a year, he was dead at the young age of 57. His daughter Anne won a seat for the PDs in the 1987 general election, though not in Dublin Central.

It says something about Ahern's political machine in Dublin Central that as a relative unknown he was able to so quickly, and so totally, come to dominate a man who, for virtually two decades, had been a serious contender for the leadership of Fianna Fáil. In his book on Fianna Fáil, *The Power Game*, Stephen Collins cites a story told by Tony Gregory, an independent Dublin Central TD, about his introduction to the bitterness of internal Fianna Fáil politics. Collins wrote: 'Gregory canvassed a row of houses not long after Ahern had done so. At one door an elderly woman, clearly a Fianna Fáil voter, gave him a better-than-expected reception. "Mr Ahern said we're to vote for him number one and Tom Leonard [also of Fianna Fáil] number two, but he told us to give you the number three, ahead of George Colley," the voter told an astonished Gregory.' The story is put into further perspective when one considers that there has never been any love lost between Ahern and Gregory. Yes, there was only ever going to be one winner of the battle between Ahern and Colley in Dublin Central.

48

Shooting the Messenger
1997

PROLOGUE

It was coming towards the end of the general election campaign of 1997 and Fine Gael was becoming extremely nervous. This was an election the party should win. It had been handed power on a plate two and a half years earlier after the collapse of the Albert Reynolds-led Fianna Fáil-Labour government. The Fine Gael leader John Bruton had surprised many people by the statesman-like manner in which he took to the job of Taoiseach. The three parties in the Rainbow coalition got on reasonably well (particularly Fine Gael and Democratic Left – who would have believed it?). The economy was performing strongly and Reynolds' successor, Bertie Ahern, had failed to convince in his role as leader of the opposition. But with general election day approaching fast, it was clear that things were not going according to plan.

The alternative government of Fianna Fáil and the PDs was ahead in the polls and it was largely down to one man – Ahern. He had metamorphosed during the campaign, shedding the half-hunted look and uncertain delivery of the previous year to put in a barnstorming performance on the hustings. Travelling by helicopter, car and bus, Ahern travelled the country canvassing in blitzkrieg fashion, shaking hands and kissing babies – and even famously one attractive young woman in Galway – as he went. He was a natural campaigner and the public he met warmed to him. The energy and vibrancy of his canvassing had to be seen to be believed and it was clearly lifting the whole Fianna Fáil campaign.

In contrast, the first two weeks of Bruton's canvass had been much more low-key. Less comfortable pressing the flesh than Ahern, Bruton wasn't helped by the fact that he had chosen to travel extensively by train, which meant he was cut off from voters along the route. His bus tour of rural areas had failed to capture the imagination of the media or the electorate; the campaign lacked *vah-vah-voom*. When he and the other two leaders of the Rainbow coalition parties, Dick Spring and Proinsias de Rossa, had a walkabout in Dublin's trendy Temple Bar, the streets seemed deserted. Bertie Ahern, meanwhile, was donning a Planet Hollywood jacket with the help of Sylvester Stallone on a stage in front of hundreds in the centre of the capital, ensuring blanket coverage in the following day's tabloids (and the broadsheets too).

THE DRAMA

Fine Gael strategists were aware that their campaign had failed to ignite. Therefore, they took a decision in the last week or so of the election to take the fight to Ahern. But it wasn't just Ahern they took the fight to. The word began to come back from Fine Gael sources that the party was unhappy that RTÉ had assigned its most senior reporter, Charlie Bird, to shadow Ahern for the entire campaign, while the highly-respected but less high-profile Joe O'Brien was on the canvass with the Taoiseach.

'Charlie Bird makes everything sound more exciting,' one Fine Gael official told *The Sunday Times*. 'He is more enthusiastic and more energetic.' They also complained that Bird's senior status as special correspondent often meant that his reports were higher up in the running order – missing the obvious point that there may simply have been more happening on the Ahern campaign trail. But it wasn't just off-the-record mutterings. Fine Gael made a formal complaint to RTÉ about the prominence Ahern was getting on its news bulletins each evening. And on RTÉ's *Questions & Answers* programme a few days before polling, Agriculture Minister Ivan Yates raised the issue. He accused RTÉ of putting out 'video promotional material on Bertie'. He alleged that Bird had not asked 'a single hard question' of the Fianna Fáil leader, engaging instead in a 'fireside chat'.

They were unwarranted charges. Bird himself refers to it in his autobiography *This is Charlie Bird*, quite correctly noting that 'Yates and his colleagues in Fine Gael would have been better served looking at how the two parties and their respective leaders managed and organised their campaigns. If they had undertaken such an exercise, they would have discovered why the campaigns were getting different treatment in the nightly television reports. I reported what I saw and Joe reported what he saw. We were just doing our jobs.'

Bird was understandably furious at what Yates had said – as was the RTÉ chapel of the NUJ which condemned 'the attempt to drag the name and reputation of a journalist into political debate' and passed a motion commending Bird's professionalism and integrity. To be fair, the highly personable Agriculture

Minister had the good grace to apologise to Bird a few days later, writing to him that 'it was never my intention to in any way impugn you personally or professionally'.

EPILOGUE

It said something about the power television enjoys over politicians that, to use Bird's words, 'senior political figures and media-watchers could seriously think that two RTÉ reporters could, on their own, influence the outcome of the general election.' There is no doubt that Bird is influential but, as he acknowledged himself, the more pertinent fact was that Ahern was leaving Bruton in his wake and was simply having a better campaign.

Fine Gael did seriously up its game in the final days of the campaign – taking on Ahern, accusing him of fudging the issues, engaging in a soundbite campaign and challenging him to public debates outside of the planned RTÉ centrepiece debate. Bruton comfortably won that RTÉ debate, but coming just 36 hours before the polls opened, it was probably too late to seriously influence the outcome.

Who knows what would have happened if Fine Gael had taken the fight to Ahern earlier, as the outcome proved tighter than some of the opinion polls had indicated. While Bruton hadn't a great campaign, the credibility he had built up as Taoiseach helped Fine Gael to a very respectable result, increasing its seat total by nine to 54. But Labour's 'Spring Tide' of five years earlier had firmly gone out – it lost 15 seats, while Democratic Left also dropped two to leave the Rainbow coalition six seats short of the Fianna Fáil / PDs total of 81. Perhaps the outcome might also have been

Shooting the messenger

different if the Rainbow coalition had gone for a spring election, when Fianna Fáil was unprepared, or an autumn polling date after the publication of the McCracken Report (see Chapter 24). But the simple truth may be that there was really no halting the Ahern juggernaut.

The story was told in one newspaper after the election that on the night of the debate, Bruton told Ahern he was lost in admiration for the way Fianna Fáil conducted its campaign. Certainly, Ahern won a general election he had no right to win, largely – though not exclusively – on the back of his personality and a soft-focus, presidential-style campaign. Television undoubtedly helped Ahern's election, but only because it captured the excitement his campaign generated. As Charlie Bird puts it: 'In truth, it was hard not to do a good job reporting on the Ahern campaign in 1997.'

49

The Indian Among the Cowboys
1992

PROLOGUE

It was late 1992 and Labour strategists were finalising candidates for the upcoming general election. Clare was one of the constituencies where the party had been unable to find somebody suitable to run. However, at a campaign meeting, general secretary Ray Kavanagh announced that the constituency had come up with both a candidate and a slogan. The candidate's name was Moosajee Bhamjee and he was a psychiatrist of Indian race who was originally from South Africa.

Fergus Finlay, who was Labour's deputy press spokesperson at the time, recounts in his autobiography, *Snakes and Ladders*, that there was a 'stunned silence' around the table. This was a time well before the Celtic Tiger experienced the large inward migration that would dramatically alter Ireland's gene pool. Anything other than a white face was still a very unusual sight on the streets of cities, towns and villages around the country.

The party's director of elections, Barry Desmond – ever the straight talker – posed the question that the others in the room were afraid to ask. According to *Snakes and Ladders*, the conversation went like this:

'Can I ask, is it fair to assume that we are talking about a black man?'

Kavanagh replied: 'Well, I think in South Africa he'd be called coloured.'

'And tell me,' Barry pressed on, fingering the note that had been faxed up from Clare, 'can it really be true that the Clare constituency is proposing to use the slogan "A vote for Moosajee Bhamjee is a vote for change"?'

Assured that it was, Barry looked around the table and said: 'I think we'd better say "yes", if only so we can claim to have produced the understatement of the campaign!'

In his own book, *Spring, Summer and Fall: The Rise and Fall of the Labour Party*, Kavanagh recalls reminding the election committee that 'the people of Clare had elected de Valera and he was an American, and what was worse, they had elected Daniel O'Connell, and he was a Kerryman!'

THE DRAMA

Not only was there no backlash against the candidature, but on 26 November 1992 – as part of Labour's sensational performance nationally – Bhamjee caused probably the shock of the election by being elected to Dáil Éireann on the eighth count. He became the State's first Muslim TD and Clare's first Labour deputy since the 1960s. It was an extraordinary performance. Dick Spring later commented that you could probably have got 1,000/1 on him the day he was nominated. While bookmakers are not renowned for giving such generous odds, there is no question Bhamjee went into that election as a rank outsider.

The Irish Times summed it up when it reported that 'the election of an ethnic Indian Muslim socialist psychiatrist to a seat in conservative Clare will be one of the great talking points of this election'. The report went on to point out that Bhamjee had only been living in Clare for ten years (although he had studied in Ireland, having arrived here in the 1960s, and was married to a local woman), noting caustically that 'working in a mental hospital does not, in itself, get out much of a vote'. Bhamjee was, however, known in the constituency through local politics and youth soccer. During that 1992 election there were also some serious local issues, such as services at the local hospital and the opposition to the proposed visitor centre for the Burren National Park at Mullaghmore, but there is no denying the importance of the Spring Tide in Bhamjee's victory.

Fergus Finlay recalls that there was a huge party in the Riverside Centre on Dublin's quays on the night of the count. Not surprisingly, the atmosphere was jubilant. The 12 Labour TDs just elected in Dublin – up three from 1989 – were there, most of them poll toppers. They all got huge cheers, as did Dick Spring when he arrived up from the count centre in Tralee. 'But the biggest cheer was reserved for the announcement, very late on, that Clare too had voted for change. Moosajee Bhamjee became the thirty-third Labour deputy elected that night,' Finlay wrote.

In January, at the Labour delegate conference to endorse the party going into government with Fianna Fáil, Bhamjee addressed the audience. As Ray Kavanagh later recalled, as a natural performer he 'had them eating out of his hand'. He told the delegates that the people of Clare had elected enough cowboys in their time and at the last election they had decided that it was now time to elect an Indian. The line will forever be associated with Bhamjee's extraordinary victory in Clare.

EPILOGUE

Ground-breaking and all as Bhamjee's victory was, it did not turn out to be the beginning of a long political career. Despite his election to the Dáil, he opted to maintain his position as consultant psychiatrist at Ennis General Hospital. And, like many first-time deputies before him, he found life as a backbencher somewhat frustrating. In his maiden speech in the Dáil, he said he hoped he would bring 'colour and flavour' to the proceedings – he certainly did that. Thanks to his straight talking, he attracted a good deal of publicity during his tenure in the Dáil. But he wouldn't have been regarded as one of the top attendees of the Dáil.

A profile in *The Irish Times* of him in 1996 wrote that 'the flying nature of his visits to the Dáil have been the subject of mirth in the chamber'. He didn't hold traditional clinics like other TDs. In 1997, faced with a choice between his medical career and politics, he opted for the former, candidly (as always) telling one newspaper that he was 'more of a doctor than a politician'. Without him on the ticket, Labour lost the seat in the election and the party hasn't come close to regaining it since.

It's hard to know how Bhamjee would have fared in the 1997 general election had he stood. Clare was never Labour heartland and the party had a disastrous election nationally compared to 1992. Furthermore, a lot of the local issues that Bhamjee had won support on five years earlier had been resolved by the time of the 1997 election. The odds would certainly have been against him, but then again they were in 1992 when nobody, least of all Bhamjee himself, expected him to become the first Indian among the cowboys.

50

Ode to Fianna Fáil
1948

PROLOGUE

Éamon de Valera founded the *Irish Press* in 1931 to offset what he regarded as the hostility of the existing media to his new political party, Fianna Fáil. Although the new paper promised not to be the 'organ of an individual or a group or a party', and its motto was 'the truth in the news', it made no secret of its editorial support for Fianna Fáil. This support was certainly one of the key forces underpinning the party's early successes.

Setting out to give ordinary people a voice, the newspaper's undoubted journalistic brilliance meant it quickly became an enormous success. As J.J. Lee put it, its 'ebullient free-wheeling polemical style outraged genteel spirits' and it played an important part in Fianna Fáil's election victories 'not only by confirming the convictions of the faithful, but also by converting previous non-voters or even unbelievers'. However, not everyone was enamoured.

Not surprisingly, Fianna Fáil's opponents disliked the paper. Noel Browne, in his autobiography *Against the Tide*, said the *Irish Press* newspapers had 'influenced a substantial number of the Irish people and created and kept unchallenged the awesome charisma of Éamon de Valera. They also contributed to the formation of the unique Fianna Fáil ethos of Irish Republicanism, particularly in rural areas.'

Meanwhile the President of the Executive Council at the time of the *Irish Press's* foundation, William T Cosgrave, accused the paper of an unrelenting campaign of innuendo against the Free State establishment. Mark O'Brien, in his book *De Valera, Fianna Fáil and the Irish Press*, wrote that 'the *Irish Press*'s populist tone succeeded in identifying Fianna Fáil with the mass of the people, while simultaneously portraying Cumann na nGaedheal as an imperial-friendly party'.

Even after Fianna Fáil assumed government in 1932, 'the *Irish Press* was the only daily paper to give any semblance of credibility to the Fianna Fáil administration. As a result of this, the paper, having originally been founded to articulate a radical populist discourse, became an organ of defence for the party,' wrote O'Brien. And by the general election of 1948, Fianna Fáil needed all the defenders it could get. The party had been in government for 16 continuous years and was under serious pressure from a new vibrant political force in Clann na Poblachta. The *Irish Press* was strong in defending the party's 16-year period in office. 'The extent to which the paper helped Fianna Fáil defend its hegemony and demonise its opposition was demonstrated by the results of an *Irish Independent* pre-election content-analysis survey. It found that, during the campaign, the *Irish Press* had devoted 76 per cent of its political column inches to Fianna Fáil, while Clann na Poblachta had received only 6 per cent,' according to Mark O'Brien.

The Clann's stance on the Irish language, partition and the link with sterling was criticised by the *Irish Press*. To be fair, much of the coverage involved straight reporting of politicians' comments.

But there were some blatantly pro-Fianna Fáil pieces, none more so that a specially written poem on the election, given special billing at the top of page five just two days before polling.

THE DRAMA

Entitled 'How Shall I Vote?' and signed 'M', the poem read as follows:

> For whom shall I vote? Aye there's the rub
> It's a problem, I must decide now
> My mind's in a whirl with all the hub-bub
> (will that loudspeaker please stop its row?)
> Slogans and catch-cries are all very fine,
> But I fear that they won't help me out,
> Nor am I impressed by speakers who whine,
> Who wheedle or bluster or shout.
>
> What I want is a policy simple and straight –
> Well Fine Gael says it has one,
> But it seems to be founded on rancour and hate,
> And on quarrels long since dead and gone
> For the rest it would say to this nation of ours
> 'Hang on to the Empire's tail!'
> But we've had some of that!
> And so, by the powers, I don't think I'll vote Fine Gael.

Then there is Labour – or rather there's two
Of the name, which compete for my vote,
But a party that's split can hardly come through
With a policy worthy of note.
As for Clann na Talmhan, I very much fear
That it will not progress very far,
Its wagon is ditched which makes it quite clear
It will never get hitched to a star.

There's another Clann left – shall I give it a name?
The Clann of the embittered men –
That broadcasts its lies without any shame
And when cornered repeats them again.
They seize upon every false rumour that goes
And out of it fashion a stick
To belabour the honour and good name of those
Whose boots they are not fit to lick.

Well that's cleared the road! So now I can walk
To the booth with an unclouded mind,
And I'll vote for the men who have done more than talk
In the dark years we're leaving behind.
For though Dev and his men may have erred now and then,
Being human, just like you and me,
Their record is there, through days foul and fair,
For the world and for Ireland to see.

EPILOGUE

Despite this poetic fervour and other subjective pieces in the *Irish Press* (there was another first-person piece entitled 'A Young Man

Says Why he will Vote Fianna Fáil'), de Valera's party did not have a very good election and lost power to the first inter-party government ('a concept disapproved of by the *Irish Press*,' according to Mark O'Brien).

While hardly objective, there is something incredibly naive and innocent about those pieces when viewed six decades on. They were certainly simpler times. An advert in the *Irish Press* for Fianna Fáil during the same campaign features a picture of a 'working man', with the headline: 'I can't even have a bottle of stout'. Warning about the need for strong government (i.e. Fianna Fáil government) to avoid sharp price increases, the advert declares 'your bottle is better and cheaper than anywhere else in the world – thanks to good old Dev'.

But the quaint and old-fashioned diction shouldn't blind anybody to the realities of elections back then. The 'Red Scare' tactics of that election (see Chapter 45) make the general elections of the recent past seem like a teddy bear's picnic. Elections in the first half century of the new Irish State were a deadly serious business, as evidenced by an advert placed by Fianna Fáil in the *Irish Press* on a number of occasions during the 1948 campaign. The ad warned that men 'purporting to act for Fianna Fáil' were canvassing in Rathmines in Dublin and threatening voters with dire consequences if they didn't vote for Fianna Fáil. It stressed that these people had no authority to speak on behalf of Fianna Fáil and that voters should contact the party if they came across them.

Of course, elections weren't a matter of life or death – they were far more important than that.

51

Death on the Canvass – 3
1948

PROLOGUE

Elections since the year dot have experienced the phenomenon of dead people voting (not literally of course). However, the idea of the electorate voting for a dead person is a lot more unusual. Yet that is exactly what happened in one constituency in the general election of 1948.

THE DRAMA

On 3 February of that year – the day before the general election took place, John J. Keane, a 59-year-old Fianna Fáil candidate for Galway West, passed away. He had suffered a heart attack the previous night after addressing a rally at Camus in Connemara where he had told supporters: 'You are at the crossroads; follow Éamon de Valera and he will guide you along the road to truth, the road to prosperity and the road to freedom'.

Incredibly, Keane was the fourth politician to die in the course of the campaign. Three Fine Gael TDs from the previous Dáil had passed away; two in Carlow–Kilkenny and one in Sligo-

Leitrim. In Carlow-Kilkenny, the death of Eamonn Coogan had taken place after the close of nominations, so – as is the norm in these situations – polling was deferred in the constituency by six days to allow for a fresh nomination process.

However, that couldn't happen in Galway West because by the time Keane had died, voting in the islands part of the constituency had already taken place. So the election had to go ahead and, for the first time in the history of the State, voters in a constituency went to the polls to vote for a list of candidates, one of whom was dead. The possibility of the late Keane being elected to the Dáil was discussed in the national media on election day.

However, Keane polled just 2,146 votes, around half of what he had got when he failed to be elected four years earlier, and was never in the running to be elected. The three sitting TDs (two Fianna Fáil and one Fine Gael) were returned.

EPILOGUE

If Keane had been posthumously elected to the Dáil that day, it would have resulted in a by-election being held in the constituency sometime after the new Dáil met. Keane did get elected to the Dáil while alive, winning a by-election in 1940. That by-election took place against the backdrop of the deaths while on hunger strike of two IRA men. At the inquest into the deaths of the two men, counsel for the prisoners' families Seán MacBride (future leader of Clann na Poblachta), during his cross-examination of the Justice Minister Gerald Boland, claimed that the whole country was against letting the men die. Boland replied that the forthcoming by-election in Galway would prove otherwise.

Fine Gael stood aside for the by-election and the result was seen as an endorsement of the government's tough line: Keane was elected with 72 per cent of the vote, defeating Clann na Talmhan's Michael Donnellan. However, Keane narrowly lost his seat in the general election of 1943 and failed to regain it a year later in 1944.

52

Safety in Number(One)s
1977

PROLOGUE

There are four words that should never, ever be used in polite conversation with a TD and they are: 'Your seat is safe.' It doesn't matter if he or she has topped the poll in every election since entering politics, no politician, even (or maybe particularly) Bertie Ahern, wants to hear those words. Being seen as 'safe' means that supporters don't necessarily have to get to the polling station to cast their vote or, worse still, they might opt to vote for somebody else on the party ticket. Politicians will do anything to convince voters that, far from being safe, their seat could be in danger, including in one famous case, putting an ad in the local newspaper to that effect.

THE DRAMA

Fianna Fáil TD Tom McEllistrim had topped the poll in Kerry North in the general elections of 1969 and 1973 (and before that his father, also Thomas, had been elected for the constituency in every election since 1923). But in the days leading up to the 1977 general election, Tom wasn't a happy man. The word was out that his seat was, of all things . . . safe. Drastic measures were called for. He decided to break ranks with his party and make a personal appeal to voters. McEllistrim took out an ad in *The Kerryman* newspaper with the following message: 'There is a rumour going around the constituency to the effect that my seat is safe. Many of my voters might be inclined to vote for one or other of the Fianna Fáil candidates on that account. I think that is a mistake. My seat could be in danger, due to the fact that we have three candidates this time. I would like to appeal to all my voters to come out and vote for me if they want me elected.'

Not surprisingly, Fianna Fáil HQ were not exactly thrilled at McEllistrim's move. The party was going all out to win two out of the three seats in Kerry North. The belief within Fianna Fáil was that this could only be done if there was a better spread of votes across its candidates, rather than McEllistrim being way out in front as happened in 1973. For this reason, the party had decided to run three candidates, with newcomer Denis Foley drawing support from the same part of the constituency as McEllistrim.

On hearing about the advert, Fianna Fáil HQ instructed local director of elections Jack Lawlor to ensure the ad did not run. However, his hurried attempt to have it cancelled failed because, as *The Kerryman* later put it, the advert was placed by Tom McEllistrim and could 'not be removed without his say-so'. Lawlor left *The Kerryman* offices 'to find his erring candidate', the newspaper reported. Later it was learned that Lawlor did catch up with McEllistrim only to be told that the advert had been approved by Fianna Fáil's Dublin election HQ. This was denied by what *The Kerryman* described as an 'authorative party source'. To counter McEllistrim's ad, the Kerry North Fianna Fáil organisation placed its own advert in *The Kerryman*, which ran on

52 – Safety in Number(One)s

the same page. Signed by Jack Lawlor, it read: 'Any advert which does not contain the names of the three candidates has not the approval of the national director of elections. I appeal to the voters of North Kerry to support our candidates on the basis of winning two seats by voting 1, 2, 3 in the order of your choice for Kit Ahern, Denis Foley and Thomas McEllistrim'.

The Kerryman, quite naturally, reported on the goings-on over the ad in a news story headlined: 'Mac kicks the party traces'. It pulled few punches in its coverage, rubbishing the suggestion that McEllistrim's seat might be in danger and stating that his actions had endangered Fianna Fáil's chances of a second seat. 'There is no profit in it for Fianna Fáil if Tom McEllistrim does too well in first preferences, whatever it might do for Tom's ego,' the report said. It added that McEllistrim's 'instinct for going it alone is well recognised. He did it in 1969 when the joint canvass of Tralee broke down, and he did it in 1973 when he invaded Kit Ahern's end of the constituency.'

There was a determination in Fianna Fáil that no member of the ticket would do his or her own thing this time and HQ was to be called in if there was any suggestion of that, the newspaper report said. Which is exactly what happened when news emerged of McEllistrim's advert.

Ironically, before he was aware of the ad, Jack Lawlor had issued a statement praising Fianna Fáil's three 'outstanding candidates who have made up the finest team in the country' and had 'worked together tremendously well'. Apart from, of course, when they quite clearly weren't 'working together tremendously well'.

EPILOGUE

As is so often the case when there is a spat between candidates from the same party, there was no damage to the Fianna Fáil vote (all publicity being good publicity). Quite the contrary – the party succeeded in winning two seats, although this may have had more to do with the national landslide for the party than any increased profile for the candidates as a result of the row over McEllistrim's ad. McEllistrim predictably topped the poll, although his share of the vote was down five percentage points from 1973 and just a couple of hundred votes ahead of running mate Kit Ahern.

Denis Foley got a very respectable 5,329 votes and his transfers elected his two running mates. The three-candidate strategy had worked and, in a show of unity, the three were chaired around the count centre when the result was announced. But the unity was short-lived. When it came to his victory speech, McEllistrim made no mention of Denis Foley. Their political rivalry was only just beginning. For the following three elections, both Foley and McEllistrim succeeded in getting elected but after that it was a case of 'one or the other'. In 1987, McEllistrim lost out (by just four votes to Labour's Dick Spring) only to regain his seat at Foley's expense in 1989. In 1992, however, Foley was returned with McEllistrim losing out in that election and in 1997. Their legendary rivalry is now continued by their offspring. Tom McEllistrim III comfortably held off a challenge from Norma Foley to hold his seat in the 2007 general election. Spanning two generations, the McEllistrim–Foley head-to-head record in Kerry North reads as follows: Played nine: McEllistrim wins three, Foley wins three, and three draws (when both were elected).

53

Browned-Off Bertie
2007

PROLOGUE

It was the first week of the 2007 general election campaign and Bertie Ahern was having a bad time of it. His dream of becoming the first Taoiseach since de Valera to win three consecutive elections seemed to be slipping away from him. The previous autumn, the Taoiseach not only survived but emerged stronger from revelations that he had received money – a mixture of loans and gifts – when Minister for Finance in the early 1990s. However, the calling of the general election in May 2007 coincided with leaks from the Mahon Tribunal in relation to Bertie Ahern's personal finances that raised fresh questions about the Taoiseach. The revelations concerned a payment of roughly STG£30,000 in cash given to Ahern by Manchester-based businessman Michael Wall in December 1994. The two men have said the cash was intended to fund work on a house in Drumcondra, which was in the process of being purchased by Wall to be rented by Ahern. Ahern later purchased the house from Wall.

The issue of Ahern's finances dominated the opening days of the Fianna Fáil campaign, which seemed in crisis. It didn't help matters that the Taoiseach was pretty much declining to answer questions on what had emerged in the leaks. On the Thursday after Bertie Ahern's Sunday dawn dash to Áras an Uachtaráin to seek a dissolution of the Dáil, Fianna Fáil launched its manifesto in the historic Round Room of the Mansion House, where the first Dáil convened in 1919. A key proposal in the manifesto was the abolition of stamp duty for first-time house buyers. In a normal election this would have been a big story. But this was no ordinary election. The manifesto launch was supposed to show Fianna Fáil at its best: confident, upbeat, professional, the party of government. It certainly didn't achieve that, but it did produce 12 minutes of an extraordinary press conference.

THE DRAMA

For about 20 minutes, everything went relatively smoothly. There was a slick video presentation after which the Taoiseach and Tánaiste Brian Cowen emerged to give their presentations. Ahern, flanked by the entire cabinet, delivered his speech and then responded to questions from the media – some about the manifesto, others about his finances, which he swatted away.

But then Vincent Browne, well-known journalist and barrister, seated among the rows of journalists directly in front of where the Taoiseach stood on the podium, grabbed the microphone. A quiver of apprehension could be felt throughout the large room. And it was not misplaced. What followed was a forensic and highly detailed interrogation of Bertie Ahern that only Vincent Browne, with his mixture of insightfulness and bloodymindedness, could have delivered.

In boxing parlance, Browne opened with his gloves down by his side, barely sparring – 'my first question has nothing to do with the planning tribunal' – before unleashing a formidable right hook: 'When you were making full disclosure of your financial dealings last September, in your interview with Bryan Dobson on RTÉ and in your subsequent Dáil statements, why did you not disclose then that you received £30,000 from Michael Wall in your office in St Luke's on the 2nd of December 1994; that was three days before you were expected to be elected Taoiseach for the first time? Nothing to do with the tribunal'.

Ahern, shifting uneasily in the podium like a witness in a courtroom drama, initially tried to fend off Browne's question by using the Tribunal confidentiality requirement to justify why he was not able to answer questions on the issue. 'Vincent, I will deal with all those issues but that money was not money for me. It was money for his affairs [Michael Wall], in his house. I hope that answers the question'.

But the Taoiseach must have known Browne, of all people, wasn't going to buy that. 'No it doesn't,' replied the veteran reporter and broadcaster. 'First of all you took the money and put it in your own bank safe and secondly it was lodged in the account of your then partner. So this was money that either you or your partner then received. Now why didn't you tell us about this last September when you were purportedly revealing all?'

Ahern responded that he 'revealed last year all of the issues that were relevant to me. The money you are talking about and the money that has been in the public domain was his money [Michael Wall], money administered by Celia Larkin on his behalf. And I think nobody wants this issue, all of these issues, resolved more than me. But my view, Vincent, is there is a place to do this. That's in the tribunal. From my point of view I think the Irish people deserve a campaign on issues. This tribunal is not about my affairs. It is about whether I received money from Owen O'Callaghan, or did I do something about blocking Quarryvale. That is nothing to do with money that was given by a person who was purchasing a house I subsequently rented. There is no accusation against me whatever about Michael Wall or about renting a house.'

But Browne was undeterred. '... The issue I am exploring is to do with the £30,000 and apparently you are alleging, or you are claiming, that the £30,000 was for the renovation of a house in which you were putting £50,000 towards that, a total of £80,000 for the renovation of a house that was worth no more than £140,000 or £150,000 when the house was only three or four years old at the time. Your credibility comes into question in that regard. What were you doing committing to put £50,000 into the renovation of a house you were purporting merely to rent, albeit with a purchase option? A lot of people don't find it credible that that money was for the purpose – £80,000 for the purpose of renovation of a house worth about £140,000, a four-year-old house'.

By this stage, despite being under intense scrutiny, Ahern's body language was starting to change – almost as if, despite himself, he was relieved to be able to face the charges head on: 'Well, Vincent you read the transcript, obviously; that is quite clear. And, as you know, that isn't what was spent on the house . . . Vincent, I have given all of the details to the tribunal and I have explained that. That was not my money. It was Mr Wall's money administered by Celia Larkin and I have given all the details on that. The issues that I gave out last year were the issues that were my money and I have given all of those details, Vincent, and the rest of the questions I will deal with at the Mahon tribunal'.

There had been gentle efforts to coax back the microphone from

Browne and pass it to somebody else to ask a question. But Browne was having none of it. Then Fianna Fáil's director of elections, the legendary PJ Mara, formerly a close associate of Charlie Haughey, attempted to intervene, calling 'Vincent . . . Vincent', signalling to him to wrap up. But again Browne brushed off the efforts. 'I am sorry PJ. Might I remind PJ that 20 years ago at Fianna Fáil press conferences we attempted to press the then leader of Fianna Fáil on his financial affairs and we were obstructed in doing so. We were obstructed in doing so again in 1989 and I hope Fianna Fáil has changed and there won't be obstruction in doing so now. The problem about this money that you got from Michael Wall is that it ain't credible that it is for the purposes of the renovation of a house. The house is a new house. You are saying that £30,000 was for the renovation of a new house worth only four times that, and that he was going to rent that house to you for merely £450 a month and that in addition you were going to put £50,000 into the renovation of a house you weren't going to own at that time.'

But Ahern also had the bit between his teeth: 'If you read the transcript, which you obviously did, it shows precisely that he spent some money on the house. But it's his money and his house . . . surely I am not responsible. If Vincent Browne bought the house and Vincent Browne got somebody to administer money for that house and that person administers the money on that house and the bills are all sent to a tribunal. All the bills relating to that money were all given to a tribunal . . . therefore, should I be answering that? That is an unreasonable position.'

Browne again asked why Ahern put £50,000 into the renovation of a house he was merely going to rent.

'Because,' replied the Taoiseach, 'if I have money in my own account, Vincent, and I want to have money to do something in my own accounts – within my own savings – what is wrong with me doing that? ... Let's be frank about this; this has nothing to do with the tribunal. Michael Wall and Celia Larkin, in my view – nothing to do with the tribunal. When I allocated my money for uses ... I'm entitled to do that. I earned the money. I got some of it from friends. It was my money.'

EPILOGUE

It was sensational stuff. Everybody in the Mansion House that day had the feeling that, yet again in that famous room, history was being made. Ok, it wasn't quite at the level of the first Dáil or the Dáil debates after the Treaty (or even close) but, by the standards of the recent elections, this felt like a big deal. The initial response from many was that the manifesto launch had been an unmitigated disaster for Fianna Fáil. The glossy, promise-laden manifesto had been swamped by the real issue – the Taoiseach's finances.

But even at the time, and certainly later, there were others who took a different view. The Taoiseach had thrown off the self-imposed shackles and engaged on the key issue of his finances and, despite extremely tough and knowledgeable questioning, he hadn't done at all badly. Ahern always does best when he throws off the inhibiting cautious approach he normally adopts. He seemed liberated for the first time in weeks and visibly grew in confidence as the interrogation went on. Of course, there were some inconsistencies in what the Taoiseach had said. But despite some 'loose threads' as one newspaper the next day generously described them (when is there ever not with Bertie Ahern?), there was a feeling that Ahern had perhaps turned a corner – assuming of course, as the *The Irish Times* put it, there wasn't 'some other runaway train coming down the tracks this weekend'.

Another commentator got to the nub of the issue: 'The media will parse and analyse and point out the many holes and inconsistencies. But the wider public out there may come to a radically different conclusion. Ahern was robust. In the bits shown on TV he came across comparatively strongly. The public aren't as forensic or exacting, and are also more forgiving – as events of last October proved. He may have done just enough to draw a line under it for good.'

Writing in *The Sunday Tribune*, PR-expert Terry Prone argued that it was a 'hell of a performance' and a potential turning point. She wrote that the encounter showed Ahern 'giving a more vivid and authentic performance than he had given months earlier to [Bryan] Dobson. There was real engagement, with the Taoiseach demanding that Browne acknowledge Bertie's right to do whatever the hell he wanted with his own money. He wasn't tetchy, doing the miserable little snaps he does when he's not quite in the right, but knows he isn't fully in the wrong. He wasn't maudlin and emotionally manipulative. He was straightforwardly mad as hell, sure of his facts and concentrated on ramming them straight down the Browne neck.'

There would be other 'turning points' in the campaign, arguably more important ones. Ahern finally came out and gave a very detailed statement about his finances, nearly two weeks before polling day. Again there were unanswered questions. However, given the opposition party's reluctance to risk electoral damage by being seen to go after Ahern on this issue and a feeling that the electorate was less engaged by the story than the media, it largely killed off the Taoiseach's finances as an issue in the final ten days of the campaign. Ahern's statement came a week after the PDs' embarrassing climb-down on leaving government over the weekend of 5/6 May, which did serious damage to the PDs and seemed to further focus minds within Fianna Fáil that the issue of the Taoiseach's finances had to be dealt with head-on. Brian Cowen, in his role as Finance Minister, grabbed the campaign by the scruff of the neck and this was also a factor in Fianna Fáil's increase in its opinion-poll ratings in the final two weeks of the campaign. But the main 'turning point' was, of course, Ahern's comprehensive win in the televised debate against Kenny a week before polling. Given the lack of track record relative to Ahern's ten years as Taoiseach, Kenny needed to win that debate, but he fell well short. Despite a good and confident start, Kenny clearly lost the segment of the debate on health – supposedly where the government was weakest – and it was largely downhill thereafter.

But of all the dramatic events in what was the most exciting election campaign in at least a generation, nothing matched the 12 or so minutes in the Mansion House when the best-known politician and one of the best-known journalists of their generation locked horns.

54

The Mole at the Polls
1973

PROLOGUE

Pretty much everything is fair game at election time. All sorts of tactics have been tried during campaigns: physical intimidation of candidates was a factor in the early Dála (see Chapter 5), 'Red Scares' against the non-existent hordes of Irish communists have been whipped up (see Chapter 45), the 'Green Card' of Irish patriotism has been played (see Chapter 44) and the electorate has even been warned not to switch horses mid-stream during an election in the middle of the Second World War.

In 1965, two weeks before polling day, Seán Lemass brilliantly eliminated the threat of a Fine Gael-Labour alliance by out of the blue stating that Fianna Fáil would not enter into coalition with Labour in the event of a hung Dáil. Nobody, least of all Labour, had suggested such a coalition was possible, but Lemass knew what he was doing. Labour leader Brendan Corish took the bait, declaring the next night that Labour would not go into coalition with any party. That effectively ended Fine Gael's slim hopes of forming a government and cleared the way for a Fianna Fáil return to power.

However, of all the tactics used in elections, perhaps the most unusual was Labour's secret weapon in the 1973 general election – it had a spy in the Fianna Fáil camp.

THE DRAMA

Forewarned is forearmed, as the old saying goes, and in 1973 it certainly proved relevant. On 5 February, Jack Lynch caught the opposition parties completely unawares by calling an election for the end of February. Firstly, these parties, particularly Fine Gael, were still licking their wounds over the huge divisions created by the Fianna Fáil government's Offences Against the State Bill in November. Labour and the liberal wing of Fine Gael had opposed the hard-hitting legislation, but Fine Gael leader Liam Cosgrave backed it and he seemed to be on the verge of being deposed as leader because of his stance until bombs, widely suspected to be loyalist, went off in Dublin and his party swung behind him and the Bill. Secondly, talks between Fine Gael and Labour regarding a potential coalition deal, which had been ongoing for the previous 15 months, had stalled. Cosgrave's frustrated comment that 'these talks are going nowhere. We might as well end them' had been leaked to Lynch, who, (fore)armed with this knowledge, decided the opposition's difficulty was Fianna Fáil's opportunity and called an election.

However, while Lynch benefited from that leak, the two opposition parties had even more success in getting access to highly sensitive material. In his definitive book on Fianna Fáil, *The Power Game*, Stephen Collins referred to 'a spy within Fianna Fáil' in that election. Collins wrote that 'Brendan Halligan, then general secretary of the Labour Party, confirmed in 1996 that the coalition parties knew in advance of major Fianna Fáil announcements and were in a position to take counter measures, but he refused to disclose the identity of the mole, apart from saying it was not a member of the cabinet.'

Collins identifies the Fianna Fáil decision to abolish rates on domestic dwellings (a major policy U-turn) less than a week before polling as one key example on which the opposition was forewarned. Whether it is coincidence or not, television footage of the campaign shows Brendan Halligan very, very confidently predicting, at an election rally, that Fianna Fáil would in the coming days make a major announcement to try and claw back some of the ground it had lost after a poor campaign. It was almost as if he knew something!

Fianna Fáil's finance whizz Martin O'Donoghue had come up with a plan to splash £30 million a year – the amount that would be saved on agricultural subsidies because of Ireland joining the EEC. Alerted by their Fianna Fáil informant about the package, a preemptive speech was prepared for Cosgrave to deliver, detailing how the incoming coalition would spend the £30 million a year saved because of EEC membership. This 'threw the Fianna Fáil leaders into confusion,' wrote Collins, 'but they decided to go ahead by emphasising a small number of items from what had originally been a detailed package.' Fianna Fáil opted to focus on the complete abolition of rates on domestic dwellings, announcing it just days before polling. Despite its enormous attractions as a policy, the forewarned opposition parties calmly opted to hang tough and not get lured into last-minute auction politics.

EPILOGUE

Brendan Halligan described Lynch's *volte face* on rates as 'the defining moment of the campaign'. However, Stephen Collins argues that while Lynch's opponents may have regarded it as capitulation, the move helped to revive the Fianna Fáil campaign. In the end the outcome of the election was extremely tight. Fine Gael and Labour secured a narrow majority over Fianna Fáil who polled a very respectable 46.2 per cent of the vote. The key factor in the coalition's victory was a voting pact between the two opposition parties which hadn't existed four years earlier. But the advance warning of the government's electoral strategy, thanks to their very own spy in the Fianna Fáil camp, no doubt also played a part in the victory.

55

The Dancing PDs
2007

PROLOGUE

Since the foundation of the first Dáil, there have been numerous examples of general elections resulting from the collapse of a government – in 1951, 1954, 1957, 1982 (twice), 1987 and 1992. Not surprisingly, there has never been a case of a government collapsing immediately after an election has been called, but it came very close to happening in 2007.

The twenty-ninth Dáil was within a few weeks of running its full five-year course when Bertie Ahern visited Áras an Uachtaráin bright and early on Sunday, 29 April to seek the dissolution of the Dáil. After ten very harmonious years in coalition together, Fianna Fáil and the PDs were fighting the election on the basis that their first preference was to continue in government together.

However, there was a very significant cloud on the horizon in the form of the Taoiseach's personal finances. Fresh revelations relating to Ahern's dealings with the Mahon Tribunal had emerged on the very day that the election was called, and the early days of the election campaign – including an explosive encounter between Bertie Ahern and journalist Vincent Browne at the launch of the Fianna Fáil manifesto (see Chapter 53) – had been dominated by the issue. The PDs, after a decade in government with Ahern and having stood by him when the issue of his finances first broke in autumn 2006, seemed to have little choice but to hang in there despite the media onslaught. It was a nerve-wracking time for the junior coalition partner. The party was used to being written off going into elections but this time it did seem to be in genuine difficulty. Opinion polls showed their rating as low as 2% and of their eight TDs, only one (Mary Harney) was regarded as being in any way safe. However, despite these pressures and the hullabaloo surrounding the Taoiseach's finances, the Tánaiste and PD leader Michael McDowell was sticking to the line that he did not want to turn himself into a 'mini-tribunal'; that it was the responsibility of the Mahon Tribunal to investigate and make its findings and that he wanted to concentrate on the real issues in the election.

THE DRAMA

By Friday, at the end of the first week of campaigning in May 2007, the PDs had undergone a serious U-turn on the issue of the Taoiseach's finances. The party held a press conference to launch its health manifesto at around lunchtime that day, but it was the well-being of the government that emerged as the big story.

When asked if, on the basis of his current level of knowledge, he would form a new coalition with Fianna Fáil or he would first require greater clarity from the Taoiseach on his financial affairs, McDowell surprised reporters by saying that he needed time to 'reflect' on what he referred to as new 'material' about Ahern's finances. 'This is material now coming into the public domain that changes the position. I believe that there are a number of things on which I would want to reflect. I don't want to say more than that at this stage'.

This new material, it emerged in the following days, referred to some 'explosive', according to some well-placed sources, documents that McDowell had received through his special advisor, from a journalist with a Sunday newspaper. The material in the documents was believed to comprise Mahon tribunal papers, including a copy of a full transcript of a recent interview between Ahern and the tribunal lawyers about the Taoiseach's house. McDowell was said to be 'shocked and horrified' at the material, as it convinced him that Ahern had not given him the full picture of his personal finances during the previous autumn's crisis. He shared the details of what he had discovered with Mary Harney and Liz O'Donnell immediately prior to that Friday's press conference and it was later suggested in some reports that the three agreed in principle that their party could not remain in government with Fianna Fáil. The reports suggested that they decided to sleep on the matter and consult with other party colleagues before finalising a decision on what would be a highly dramatic course of action.

The following morning's newspapers were full of speculation about the PDs' future in the outgoing government. That day's *Irish Times* also disclosed further information about Ahern's dealings with the tribunal, including queries about a number of foreign-exchange transactions in the 1990s. The speculation about the future of the government intensified as the day went on. On the campaign trail in Longford that day, McDowell notably refused the opportunity to play down the gravity of the situation. He described the situation as serious and confirmed a meeting of senior PD figures would take place that afternoon. By this stage, television and radio reports were stating that the PDs were on the brink of pulling out of government.

A grim-faced Taoiseach, when asked about McDowell's comments, said the Tánaiste 'needed to do what he needed to do'. Privately, Fianna Fáil figures were resigned to losing their long-time coalition partner. Perhaps emboldened by news that an opinion poll in the following day's *Sunday Business Post* showed Fianna Fáil recovering support and the PDs not doing well, one source caustically asked: 'Is this the 2007 version of McDowell going up the lamp post?' (see Chapter 12). On RTÉ's *Six-One* news, reporter Charlie Bird stressed that there was 'no smoking gun' in the new material given to McDowell, but it was the totality of the information which had alarmed McDowell and provoked the response.

Meanwhile, the four senior figures in the PDs – McDowell, Harney, O'Donnell and party president Tom Parlon – were meeting in the Kildare home of PD senator John Dardis. Other members of the parliamentary party seemed to be in the dark about what was going on, but it was clear even by Saturday evening that not everybody was enthused by the idea of pulling out of government. There was a real concern at grassroots level that it would be seen as a meaningless gesture that also could be counterproductive, losing the party vital transfers from Fianna Fáil. There were also fears that withdrawal from government would leave the PDs without any coalition options, running a real risk of rendering them irrelevant facing into the general election. These people began to make their voices heard. 'The feeling now is that it's too late to do that [pull out of government]. You would be playing into the hands of the opposition,' one well-placed source said.

But by late Saturday evening, it was regarded as pretty much a given by the media that the PDs would pull out of government.

The full details of what happened at the three-hour meeting in the home of John Dardis have never emerged, but the widespread belief is that Tom Parlon – who was not impressed at having to break away from canvassing to attend the meeting – argued strongly against pulling out of government. After the Kildare meeting concluded at 7.30pm, a statement was issued by the PDs stating that the meeting had been convened to 'evaluate new information' relating to the Taoiseach's financial affairs. 'The discussion analysed the import of information relating to the purchase of Mr Ahern's home. It was agreed that the new information is highly significant. The PD leadership has now decided to enter into a a wider consultation with members of its parliamentary party.' It quickly became clear that, backed by a majority of the parliamentary party, Parlon's view had held sway. By late Saturday night, the word was coming back that there would be no withdrawal from government. The PDs had taken the government to the very edge of the cliff, but at the last moment decided against jumping.

The following morning, McDowell – unaccompanied by any other member of his parliamentary party – held a morning press conference in Dublin's Morrison Hotel. At that meeting, McDowell did not announce any withdrawal of the PDs from government, but called on the Taoiseach to give a 'comprehensive and credible' account of his financial matters before polling day by making a full statement. 'I believe that in any democracy, elected leaders must be accountable to the people in respect of standards of behaviour and truthfulness which impinge on their public duties. I believe therefore it is essential that the Taoiseach must make a comprehensive statement addressing all the new information now in the public domain and that he must do so before the people cast their votes on May 24,' he said.

The Tánaiste hinted at the nature of his concerns when he said at the press conference that the Taoiseach told him in autumn 2006 that the purchase of his house in Drumcondra from a Manchester businessman in the 1990s was 'an arms-length transaction on commercial terms for full value'.

Later that day, the Taoiseach met with his three most senior ministers – Brian Cowen, Dermot Ahern and Micheál Martin – at Fianna Fáil election headquarters and a decision was taken that the Taoiseach would indeed make a full public statement.

EPILOGUE

The whole affair was a public relations disaster for the PDs and raised old questions about McDowell's political judgement. In a matter of a couple of days the party had flip-flopped from being happy to go into government with Fianna Fáil once again, to almost pulling out of government, to stressing that it was happy to coalesce with Ahern again provided he, in his own time, delivered a statement clarifying the transactions surrounding his home in Drumcondra. Claims from the PDs that the whole thing had been blown out of proportion by the media simply had no credibility – the PDs were on the verge of bringing down the government on that Saturday.

What was truly baffling was how the PDs had allowed events to get so out of hand. McDowell's initial stance was that he was not going to turn himself into a mini-tribunal. Why did he change that stance? Ultimately, the PDs handed its political rivals a big stick with which to beat them. Fine Gael leader Enda Kenny accused the PDs of having 'no backbone', adding: 'What you have seen today is like *Lanigan's Ball*, stepping in and then stepping out.'

That weekend proved something of a turning point in the election. The heat went out of the issue of the Taoiseach's finances after that; particularly once he gave his detailed statement a week later. The PDs, given the popularity of the Health Minister Mary Harney, tried to focus on the health issue for the remainder of the campaign. However, despite a stellar performance by Michael McDowell in the debate of the leaders of the smaller parties, it wasn't destined to be a good election for the PDs. Of the big four who attended that meeting in Kildare to discuss whether or not the party would pull out of government, only Harney held her seat. McDowell quit politics on the night of the count, followed some weeks later by both O'Donnell and Parlon. The PDs were reduced to just two TDs, although Ahern's desire to build a strong government majority meant that the party was included in the new Fianna Fáil coalition government with the Green Party.

It's hard to know how big a factor the disastrous events of the weekend of the 5th–6th of May played in the party's poor performance. The strength of Fine Gael, the difficult ministries held by both Harney and McDowell, issues with party organisation, a desire for some form of change on the part of the electorate – were probably all bigger factors. But the loss of nerve at such a key time in the election campaign certainly didn't help the party's cause.